T-Time

A Rites of Passage Manual for the Adolescent Female

By

Raining Deer

authorHOUSE™

1663 LIBERTY DRIVE, SUITE 200
BLOOMINGTON, INDIANA 47403
(800) 839-8640
WWW.AUTHORHOUSE.COM

First published by AuthorHouse 03/21/05

ISBN: 1-4208-0689-0 (sc)

Printed in the United States of America
Bloomington, Indiana

This book is printed on acid-free paper.

TABLE OF CONTENTS

This text is to be used only as a guidepost towards exploring deeper meanings and more in-depth studies of cultural spiritual practices. The author and the publisher are not responsible for anything or occurrence, adverse or otherwise, resulting from the use or application of information contained in this book.

OPENING PRAYER

It is in prayer I begin this writing.
It is in prayer that I offer this gift.
It is in prayer that I share what was given to me.
It is in prayer that I step out on faith.
It is by grace that the Divine Holy Spirit has blessed me.
It is in prayer that I humbly accept the blessing.
It is in prayer that I hope the hands that find this manual,
and the eyes that read its words will receive the spirit of it
into their hearts.
It is in prayer that I request that you
make this journey with me.
It is in prayer that we shall give and restore
some goodness in the world.
It is in prayer that I ask you to share all that you learn
with those you love and know
and with those whom you do not know.
It is in prayer that I ask blessings upon you.
May you always walk in beauty
with the blessings of
The Great Spirit
and
your ancestors.

Aho. Mitakuye Oyasin.

ACKNOWLEDGMENT

I honor Thunder Horse Nokus Harjo of the Cox-Osceola Seminole Reservation, *HRH Oseijeman Adefunmi I and Chief Adenibi S. Ajamu, author Ayobunmi Sangode, and HRG Iya Orite Olasowo of Oyotunji African Village in South Carolina, Catherine Hummingbird Ramirez (the Carib Tribal Queen of Trinidad and Tobago), Denise Wilson-El of the Moorish Science Temple, The Dasa, Federal District of El-Eastmoor and I-AM Miami, Wallace Black Elk of the Lakota nation, and Minister James Shabazz and his wife Lydia for their inspiration and influence in my life. Their untiring efforts towards educating those who seek knowledge of the cultural significance of indigenous people are their legacy to our children and generations to come.

I also acknowledge and thank brother Jomo, brother Yaya Diallo and brother Douglas Spotted Eagle for their beautifully inspiring music. Spotted Eagle's *Prayer* cd - *my hymn*, and Jomo's musical purity (especially *Baqti - my anthem*) echo the voices of the ancients, and their spiritual vibrations remain a constant source of healing, balance and inspiration. I am also grateful to my *sistahs* Chipo Chemoyo, Jameelah Ahmad, Patricia Roberts, and Susan and Samantha Crook for their spirit, their dance, and their blessings. Others have walked with me, sometimes carrying me and never leaving my side on this long journey. To you I give much love -- Donzella "Mickey" Washington, Wallis and Gene Tinnie, and "Nana" Nathaniel Styles. To Philip Michael Thomas, thank you for your friendship, your encouragement, your untiring positivity -- the love and light you send my way, and for being a mirror to my soul. To Charles Thomas for sharing your love, your life --the highs

---

*On February 11, 2005, just prior to the publiaction of this book, His Royal Highness Oba Oseijeman Efuntola Adelabu Adefunmi I, (king) of Oyotunji African Village in South Carolina, performed the ultimate rite of passage and returned to his ancestors. As for those who knew him and appreciate his life's work as Father of the African Cultural Restoration Movement, we owe him a debt of gratitude and we miss his physical presence. But we say, *Peace be upon you, Kabiesi. Your new journey has begun.*

and the lows, and your family. You are simply a great partner in love. To Jude "Papaloko" Thegenus, you have been a beam of light for art and music in my life since our introduction by Tony Villate. We have shared our love for culture, for our baba Felix Morisseau-Leroy, and for justice. I always knew our work would bring us together again. Here is some of that work but I am sure there is much more to come. Thank you for being a clear channel for spirit. Mési anpil - Adupe! And finally, to Sage -- my everything, mommy loves you more than anything else in the *whole wide world*.

DEDICATION

This book is dedicated to my mother,
Retha Stephens, and to the memories of my other mother,
Aunt Doll (Willie Mae Emory), and my
Aunt Annie Mae Shinholster. All sisters, all three of the
strongest women by whom I was blessed to be raised, and who
loved me dearly. Backatcha!

"Dare to think of your humanity as something so divinely precious that it is worthy of being an offering to God."

-- Phillips Brooks

IN THIS BOOK YOU WILL FIND:

- What are Rites of Passage/T-Time

- Why we perform Rites of Passage

- The role of *ritual* and *spiritual* practices

- Tools for *prayer* and *purification*

- Introduction to Oyotunji African Village

- The *American Religious Crimes Code*

- Historical references to African and Native

  American Rites of Passage traditions

- Native Rituals: *Sweat Lodge, Vision Quest, Ghost Dance*

- The Story of *White Buffalo Woman*

- The Story *of Moremi* (Yoruba)

- *White Painted Woman* (Apache)

- *Changing Woman* (Navajo)

- Ritual Logistics

- Items needed for a Rites of Passage ceremony

- Ceremonial *Manners*

- Rites of Passage Ceremony

- Poetic tribute to women

- Resources

"There is a red river from which all life comes and it flows through all our veins. But, a woman sheds this red water every month so that life can be procreated upon the earth. As a woman, the candidate must now revere that sacred responsibility and appreciate the sacred duty given the female by God -- to have, nurture and replenish the earth with human beings..."

Raining Deer

INTRODUCTION

Since entering a new millennium, various communities across the United States seem to have become more open to applying some of the spiritual and social rituals of ancient pre-colonial societies and pre-European Native American nations. Like Kwanzaa, the *rites of passage* ritual is being adopted and integrated into coming of age celebrations like Sweet 16 festivities, birthday parties and naming ceremonies more and more each year. Many people are familiar with the *bat mitzvah* (for girls) and *bar mitzvah* (for boys) ceremonies which are performed for Jewish youth who reach the age of puberty. Likewise, other transition rituals have been performed for hundreds of years, and it is from those ancient traditions that we take direction.

While there are many forms of rites of passage rituals in various cultures, including Asian, Indian, Australian Aborigine and Pacific Island cultures, the ritual ascribed herein is a combination of some Native American and Yoruba (Nigeria, West Africa) traditions with a western flavor. There are no less than 1,300 different cultures in Africa alone and at least 500 nations are documented in America. My purpose, however, is not in any way to borrow from all of them nor to encapsulate them, but merely to give a few examples of some of their traditions and to give a basis for the method prescribed herein.

As one born of Native American and African/Moorish American ancestry (somewhat foretelling that the pathway of the ancients would find me), and having married into the Seminole family, I attained the role of spiritual interpreter (an *Iyeska* in the Lakota language). The practical translation is that during healing ceremonies I had the ability to *hear* what the ancestral spirits were saying relative to the person being healed. It could have been regarding the prescribed method of healing itself, what had caused the dis-ease in the first place, or what the person needed to do to correct an illness or a given situation. Often times, healings had more to do with a person's emotional state of unrest rather than an actual physical ailment. Mental or emotional distress will certainly manifest itself as a physical ailment if not addressed in a *positive way*. This positive way meant engaging dis-eased persons in deep meditation and then open discussion about what was bothering them.

My name, *Raining Deer* also alluded to what was to come in that I received it in a ceremony that indicated that my spirit was *as fresh as mountain rain but that being a deer and not a fawn, I had the work of a woman to do.* Mountain rain, in this instance, is representative of a higher consciousness coming through the blessing of rain -- water -- wisdom. Deer is also indicative of deer medicine, deer people, etc. (an anthropological discourse not covered in this text). Hence, *T-Time* or *Rites of Passage for the Adolescent Female.*

The purpose for the rites of passage prescribed herein is to help ward off and lessen the effects of some of the dis-ease that will befall young people living in non-traditional settings. The fact that they maybe growing up African-American, Canadian, French, German or in whatever modern society they are raised, does not negate *the need of the soul to connect with its ancient ancestral heritage.* It is within that primordial shell of spiritual connectedness that our ancestral DNA was formulated, making us who we are.

The road to rites of passage shared herein is a path on which I had embarked early in life when poetic rhymes began to filter through my mind and the other world became a silent reality for me. Frequent visions of events yet to come, future deaths, and even the coming of visitors at the precise day and time of their arrival, made me acutely aware that I had inexplicably and without effort tapped into something that no one had ever discussed with me and which, for a time, made me question by own sanity. I finally realized, however, that certain things were inevitably going to be revealed to me and that I had no control over it. I simply accepted this as a personal phenomenon and kept it to myself, not realizing at age 15 and 16 that there were many others who lived with these *gifts* and remained mum about them, until necessary occasions forced them *out*, so to speak. It was much later that I realized the enormity of the *other world* and how its presence in our current time is also real to the ancestors -- and to those who pay homage to them.

My journey became even more enlightening when I was united with Thunder Horse Nokus Harjo on the Seminole Reservation in 1990. It was in and of itself a *re-joining* of the Native American and African American. As the brothers pounded out ancient rhythms on those massive drums to which we marched -- slowly, each purposeful step consecrated in holy ground, Chief Little Dove Buford performed the ceremony. Her husband, Chief Running Buck was at her side, as was Yoruba Chief Adenibi Ajamu with Thunder Horse, [*Emperor*] Dinizulu Tinnie and his wife Wallis in their magnificent flowing robes, Shiekess Talibah Mawiyah-El, Walks Far -- a cook whom we met the first day I arrived on the reservation, other Miami and reservation elders, and my mothers looking on. One could not help but feel the ancestors showering us with their blessings. It could be said that anyone's wedding would generate the same kind of excitement and feelings of awe; however, when done in the spirit of sacred ritual, when it was set in motion within days of the wedding actually taking place (a directive from spirit), and with the will of the ancestors as the guiding force, if not the true workings of spirit, then *magic* is the only plausible explanation. But most people don't really believe in magic!

The purpose of this format is to tailor a *functional hands-on* rites of passage ritual for that portion of the American community, including Caribbean-Americans, whose lifestyles are born of western culture but who seek nevertheless to enhance the lives of their children by commemorating the heritage and the ancestral ethnicity from which they came. Some of the more basic practices traditionally performed in these kinds of ceremonies (like *animal sacrifices*, branding or scarring of the skin with *tribal marks*, suspension by the skin as in Native American *Sundance* ceremonies) will not be elaborated upon here because they require the skills of someone who has been properly trained in the medicinal arts of certain priesthoods. To point the lay person in the direction of facilitating those kinds of rituals is like sending someone who *plays* a doctor on t.v. into an actual operating room to perform bi-pass surgery. You simply cannot do that without intense and lengthy training. Otherwise, someone would end up suffering for your inadequacies.

It is however, necessary that the facilitator of a rites of passage have a firm foundation and a strong spiritual conviction about her culture and her relation to God, because that is the basis upon which she is indeed *authorized* to perform such a ritual.

As facilitator, it is not your job to try to "convert" candidates or anyone else to your way of thinking or to your culture or religion.

Most individuals already have some form of religion, whether they practice it or not. The question the candidates may end up asking themselves is *whether the ceremony resonates with their spirit -- to the very core of their being*. If it does, there may be some cultural aspect of the ceremony that they need to look into further. It could be that the facilitator will need to *refer* the candidates to a priest or medicine person of another culture altogether. The facilitator must simply remember the words of Malidoma Patrice Somé (a *medicine man* or *shaman* of the Dagara people in an area that encompasses part of northern Ghana, southern Burkina Faso and the Ivory Coast in Africa). He shared his grandfather's wisdom in his book, <u>Ritual: Power, Healing, and Community</u>, "... *The good in a service has little to do with the service itself, but with the kind of heart one brings to the task.*" Warning Somé, who was a child at the time, his grandfather, an enormously powerful medicine man, told him an unwilling heart would *"spoil a service by infecting it with feelings of resentment and anger."*

This is why it is highly *suggested* that medicine people, cultural priests and/or priestesses, or [1]shamans be sought for this kind of ceremony -- because of their training and experience. However, one should be mindful that even if a cultural priestess or medicine person is contacted and she doesn't seem to possess the *right* spirit, one must consider that perhaps she is not the proper choice, and the appropriate person has yet to reveal herself. Sometimes, as the *old ones* (ancestral spirits) say, [2]*where there is no medicine person in the village, one may be granted the authority, with the help of the ancestors, to perform the needed service for the people*, as it has been in my case.

As far as the candidates are concerned, it is not required that they live in total isolation (as in a Native American *vision quest*) for a period of time or be inducted into a school for theological study or into a women's society (like the *African Theological Archministry*

---

[1]   The term *shaman* is interchangeable with *medicine man*; however, shaman was initially from the Evenk people who speak the Tungus language in Siberia (in central and east Russia).

[2]   <u>Pulasu - *Bearing Witness to the Other World*</u>, Raining Deer, copyright 1996.

or the *Igbe Moremi Women's Society* at Oyotunji African Village in South Carolina). Today it has become necessary to *bring them over* without their going through everything that those who study the priesthood or seek theological degrees must go through. Our lives are so fast-paced and the drive for making the dollar so strong, that pursuing any cultural initiations and study can seem like insignificant distractions to youth. This is why the process should be begun, ideally (if not from birth), at the age when the desire to chase the dollar is not yet crucial to the existence of the youth so that their focus can be momentarily captured and placed on their spiritual well-being.

Although, if one has the opportunity to engage in a vision quest or in cultural theological study, such a course is recommended and, for some, it is imperative that they have more in-depth spiritual work performed for them.

We recognize today that the masses of people probably will not go into strict, lengthy regimens of training and practice of ancient ways that are new to them but, if given some basic tools, they may be gently guided into utilizing some of the rituals that have helped our fore-parents give birth to strong people and their enduring legacies. It is for that same reason that I have included a minimal amount of information and perspectives about rituals and rights of passage from a few diverse cultures.

One does not have to attend four years of college to perform or participate in a rites of passage ceremony, but it does help to have a basic understanding from indigenous people whose entire existence was built around and rooted in ceremony and ritual.

WHAT IS T-TIME?

In short, *T-Time* is simply a catch phrase for *transition time*. This can be any period of time in life when a person is moving from one level to another, which is generally the time when a *rites of passage* ceremony is called for. While this text specifically deals with the time when teenage girls begin their transformation to young womanhood, *T-Time* can be used to designate other transition times for males and females, young and old. Puberty is a period of transition for both boys and girls. Likewise, menopause is a transition time for women in their post-child bearing years, usually in their late forties or early fifties (though it can occur in women in their twenties and thirties, in which case they would experience a T-Time earlier than the norm). Entering a marriage is also a transition time, as is divorce. The ultimate transition time of life is of course - death.

When we open up to the concept that *we are spiritual beings having a human experience*, then we realize that rites of passage connect earthly beings to the spiritual realm in a way that allows for a natural interaction between the two. In traditional cultures there is no separation -- the "spirit"ual aspect of life is as important as the physical, and must always be taken into account. In fact, among the Dagara of West Africa, a person has a *double* -- meaning an *unseen* body or *other side* of the person. Diviners know how to communicate with that part of someone. But, when there has been an extreme trauma in people's lives which cause great emotional distress, they sometimes get separated from their double. Though their physical body is there and can speak and function like any other (albeit often in somewhat of a violent or confusing manner), their double is missing, and the diviners have to find it and reconnect them.

A personal experience that I had which confirmed the ability of diviners for me was in 1991 when I was in a very early stage of pregnancy -- so early that I had not mentioned my suspicion that I was pregnant to anyone, including my husband. One Sunday I had decided that the night's dinner would include succotash, a blend of lima beans and corn which I always loved when I was growing up. I wasn't sure if it was the light buttery flavor that drew me to it or the splash of springtime that danced from the bright yellow and green of the corn and beans.

Nevertheless, I was looking forward to dining, when my husband called to me from the bedroom. "Raining Deer, pick up the phone," he directed. While I was perplexed because I had not heard the phone ring, I picked up the receiver in the kitchen where I was cooking. On the other end was Chief Ajamu, a Yoruba priest and family friend who, unbeknownst to me, had been in the process of divining for my husband over the telephone.

"*Alafia*," I said, which means hello in the Yoruba tongue. "Yeah," he responded in an unusually hasty tone. There is generally a scratchy tone to Chief Ajamu's distinctive voice, and under normal circumstances, to have a conversation with him is like joining the members of a family on their porch in the southern countryside, while they're busy watching the watermelons grow. There is the introduction, pleasantries exchanged that inquire about the families, a few chuckles about the kids or some dubious character whom everybody knows, etc., etc. But this time, Chief Ajamu was in the middle of a reading and was being compelled to deliver a message to, of all people -- me. And I hadn't even asked for it.

"I was giving Thunder Horse a reading but something came through for you. They said that several eggs had been fertilized but that the witches keep taking them." Now, at that particular time, I had only been married for about eight months. My perception of witches was probably as much a Wizard of Oz concept as anybody else -- there are good witches and there are bad witches. Whether they were from the west or the east wasn't really a part of my psyche -- at least not consciously. But when he continued, had I not been a follower of my spiritual path, I would literally have been floored at the profundity of the message, and I was -- anyway, just from the clarity of the confirmation.

"They want an offering of corn and lima beans in order for them to leave the eggs alone." I chuckled, as I stirred the pot of lima beans and corn on the stove, and responded, "Okay. I'll put it right out." Without missing a beat, I served up a hefty plate of the tasty vegetables and placed them under a tree in the backyard. In a few days I announced to my husband that we were expecting.

This is only one of many such occurrences which, in their small but profound way are in essence *rites of passage* which I have gone through time after time. Early on it was without my even being aware, but later I came to understand them and then to channel the necessity for certain rites to be performed.

Primitive versus Contemporary

In this text, while we are not advocating the use of the more primitive (meaning earlier - not lesser) rituals like animal/blood sacrifice, body mutilation and the like (and we are also not drawing a conclusion as to the validity of either of these methods), we point out that the starkness of such rituals is so sharp a contrast to daily life that we should give thoughtful and thorough consideration when advising as to the study and even observance of them. To our advantage, we can utilize ritualistic methods that are more palatable to the diverse sensitivities across various communities in the west, while acknowledging the benefit of having such a rich history of life altering rituals.

T-Time is *one* practical solution for lessening the chances that children will become *separated from their double*. It is our quest to give urban and suburban youth a proper platform to propel them into young adulthood in a meaningful way that grounds them, or gives them a foundation and, which at the same time, educates those who attend such an occasion. We hope that such a profound familial celebration of life will result in generations of young people segwaying from adolescence into adulthood with the blessings of their elders and families, the wisdom of their ancestors, the guidance of their spiritual teachers and the praise of their social mentors and allies.

In many traditional cultures, when a child is born, a naming ceremony will be performed several days (eight days for the Akan) after the birth. The medicine person or priest who performs the ritual will divine on the child to determine what spiritual attributes are attached to it. Once this is done in the presence of the parents, it will be clear what is the child's purpose for coming into human form on the earthly plane. The baby's new spiritual name given at that time will indicate to others of that particular culture the attributes that were revealed in the divination process.

When my son was born in 1992, he had two naming ceremonies -- one Native American performed seven days after the birth, by my husband and myself. It was a private ritual wherein we buried the child's umbilical cord in our yard next to my teepee and near my husband's Hogan (prayer house). We knelt, with the baby in my arms, in the area which was protected by a short fence made of pieces of dense bark and was topped by a buffalo skull. Various herbs and gifts to the Earth Mother were buried with the cord as we sung prayers of thanks and requested blessings upon our child. His name came from the ancestors in another language that meant *Sage is the flower of the ancestors.*

The Yoruba ceremony was a more public presentation, though the divination was done privately. A priest revealed the name to be *Okanbe Ogunbade*, meaning *Ogun* (the Yoruba god of iron) *receives a crown.* This meant that my son would have the attributes of a person born under the aspects of Ogun. All my closest friends gathered for the ceremony. Children huddled on the white lamb-skin rug in front of a large adobe fireplace. Exposed wooden beams stretched across the expansive great room from which hung tied bundles of long-stemmed sagebrush. After each person held the baby and whispered his/her own pet name into the baby's ear along with a blessing, we feasted. There was a cake that read "Welcome to the Earth Mother, Sage" and it was enjoyed amid drumming and dancing.

It is these experiences that help me as I travel on this journey. When a person has gone through her rites of passage, she too has the ability to be directed by spirit on the road called *life.*

WHAT ARE RITES OF PASSAGE?

In essence a rites of passage ritual is a form of initiation into a higher level of consciousness, higher awareness, higher level of being. To point out to the unsuspecting youth that it is time for them to start the process of *becoming* who they are they must be shown it is necessary for them to leave their childhood behind. Some will want to live in a perpetual state of infancy and will fight the process. They must be made to understand that it is only of consequence to them if they are totally unwilling, because prisons and mental hospitals are filled to the brim with people who refused to grow up and take responsibility for themselves. Their confidence should be boosted by your encouraging them to ensure that they have a better future because of their commitment to going through with the rites of passage ceremony.

When young men or young women, in traditional societies and cultures (Native American, African, Aborigine, Asian, Hindu, etc.) reach a certain age that comes around or during the onset of puberty, historically it is widely recognized that some form of *ceremony* should be performed to mark this most important time in their young lives. These are viewed as very solemn and sacred rituals and the utmost care is taken in preparation for them and in readying the young candidates for this transition time. In the western world, these occasions are marked by Sweet 16 parties and debutante balls. But, for the indigenous, these events are not taken superficially and much emphasis is placed upon their importance, not only for the welfare of the individual candidate, but for the health of the community/village as a whole. Grave consequences are believed to overshadow the village that does not perform the necessary rituals.

In his book, *Of Water and The Spirit*, Malidoma Patrice Somé states, *"When a child grows into an adolescent, he or she **must** be initiated into adulthood. A person who doesn't get initiated will remain an* *adolescent for the rest of their life, and this is a frightening, dangerous and unnatural situation."*

From birth Somé was brought up in an atmosphere that nurtured a serious respect for the sacred and the spiritual. The idea that something *supernatural* could and *would* happen to a child who was not initiated at the proper time is distinctly different from western thinking. In America, a visiting (foreign) shaman might view the results of *non-initiations* of adolescents in a peculiar way. He/she might determine such individuals with *autistic behavior,* or *mental instability* to be victims of the non-timely initiation. Even the character of petty criminals might come under this diagnosis when they repeatedly commit misdemeanor offenses and spend time in jail rather than behaving like responsible adults who contribute to the betterment of society. In contrast, western therapists may conclude that the person in question has not "grown up," but it is probable that they would *not* attribute the cause to a *lack of ritual.*

It is thought by some that the fact that the rituals performed by indigenous people were so foreign to Europeans upon first contact, and believed by them to be heathenous acts which were against the tenets of Christianity was the reason they forced the ceremonies to be discontinued. After being practiced for thousands of years, the halting of the rituals had a critical impact upon the spiritual health of enslaved, overtaken and displaced people.

Jesuit priests even went as far as telling Somé's father that he need not concern himself with performing any rituals for his family that had been long practiced because his "ancestors had been condemned to eternal hell *and were busy burning.*" It is believed by Somé that as a direct result of the rituals not being performed by his father, whose responsibility it was to carry them out, his father lost twin daughters (who had reached puberty) within days of each other -- one from a sudden illness and the other during the funeral of her twin. Still refusing to perform the ritual, a son mysteriously passed away two weeks after the last twin. The shock of losing the twin daughters and her son caused the mother to die from grief at her son's funeral. The father suffered greatly but survived and eventually remarried. After coming close to death himself, however, he finally performed the ritual for the twins. He regained his health and fathered two more children, including Malidoma Patrice Somé, to our great benefit and joy.

This citing of *cause and effect* is basic to the premise that in nature *balance* must always be sought (even for a *group* of people bound by ethnicity and/or circumstance) and when not reached, the state of *imbalance* can have dire consequences, both physically and spiritually. From a spiritual perspective, it leads to moral decay, a general disrespect for others and disregard for life -- all of which can result in terrible karmic calamities. Therefore, rites of passage are necessary to avert the impending spiritual and physical decay, in some instances, and lack of regard for others.

Not all rites of passage rituals are so weighty. It is amusing to find that the simplest of occurrences may be used as an excuse to have a celebration. Among the Navajo, after a child is born, the females of the family who generally attend to the infant, tease the baby with their finger or a feather to instigate a smile. How many times have we heard the *oohs* and *aahs* of mothers, aunts or grandmothers upon witnessing a smile from a newborn? Deemed the *First Smile Ceremony* by the Navajo, this initial show of personality is an indication that the child has been blessed and will live a long life of contentment. Of course, the occasion is marked with a family feast which means absolutely nothing to the baby. He or she is quite happy with the mother's breast milk, or milk from whatever is the popular source of the day -- even formula. But the proud parents and family members have more opportunities to dote on their newest addition.

This ceremony may be followed by the *First Laugh* ritual, another similar type ceremony also not meant to bring the earth's rotation to a halt but, again, it lightens the spirits of those surrounding the child who will probably impact the life of the little one more than anyone.

My Village Is The World

Having gone through a number of initiations and ceremonies, I was reminded that in my own initiations, I was deemed a spiritual interpreter for my village and that *my village is the world*. Also, as stated previously, during one of my ceremonies, I was informed that my authority to perform certain rituals could be invoked where there was no medicine person directly available in a given area. This is because, in general, a woman does not become a medicine woman until she is in her mid forties. However, my T-Time rituals were performed at around age 30, giving me quite an early leap into the practice of the medicine. Because I was not brought up in a *traditional* setting, however, to have the ceremonies performed for me at 30 probably put me at the level I would normally be at had my training commenced from childhood.

From that experience I have come to understand that I and indeed -- *we* cannot afford to simply fluff off our responsibility of assisting young people in transitioning to their next level. Too much malevolence can befall them and so many are spiritually unprotected. In my own family, I have witnessed young people being separated from their souls, being caught between worlds. And I have also benefited from my elders (a grandfather and a brother) imparting to me that they were walking between realities once they had reached the stage that precedes the ultimate transition (death). I did not fully understand them at the time when they said "I'm on the other side more than here now." And selfishly I fought to keep them on this side. But after my own initiations, their words came rushing through my mind like rapids seeking an ocean to pour into. I finally understood.

Family Ritual

By the experience of Malidoma Somé in his village, the rites of passage we are addressing herein would be considered a *family ritual* which can be *semiprivate* because, while it is incumbent upon the female members of the family to perform or participate in the ceremony for the candidate, other members from the *community* may be and are usually involved. Individual rituals sort of evolve from the family rituals and community rituals, indicating how all are intertwined, as signified in the Native American phrase used to conclude a prayer, "Mitakuye Oyasin" -- we are all related. Somé encapsulates the essence of why family ceremonial rituals are performed in the most simple terms: "*The young ones are the future of the old ones. To allow this future to happen, the old ones must work with the Other-world. When an elder fails to perform his work with respect to the spiritual, the future of this elder is threatened, not the present. Where ritual is absent, the young ones are restless or violent, there are no real elders, and the grown-ups are bewildered. The future is dim.*"

I recall when I was in the latter stages of my pregnancy with my son, my spouse and I were not getting along like I would have liked, given the fact that the impending arrival of our child was right around the corner. Although we did not have knock-down drag out fights, nor did we even have very heated discussions, the tension was as thick as fat on a side of beef. I felt the need to go visit my hometown. I said my Native American prayers and sang the songs that have come to me. In my meditation the message that I got was to go home, dress up in my wedding attire, and get the blessing of the women in the family so that the child would come through safely. I did everything to the letter.

I decided that attending my mother's church services would be the best way to get the blessing of many of the family females because most of them in town would be at St. Augustine A.M.E. Zion Church on Sunday. That would also keep me from having to run all around the city trying to catch up with them. I could not have planned it better when immediately following the service my godmother, aunts, female cousins and friends all gathered around -- chatting and rubbing my stomach with good wishes, as if on cue. "Mission accomplished," I mused to myself.

When I returned to Miami, in the presence of my husband, I still felt an uneasiness, as though he wasn't quite pleased with the situation and was in some sort of denial. I contacted Chief Ajamu's wife, Iya Sangode, and asked her to divine on it.

We met at the Ilesa Anago African Temple, a spiritual base for much of the Yoruba community in South Florida. We sat down on the wine colored carpet before the temple shrine. Iya Sangode threw her shells several times and calculated what they were saying based on the ancient Yoruba system of divination. When she was finished she gave me the interpretation.

"There is some controversy surrounding this child," she began and continued with something to the affect of "You have to remember that this is your child and you have to do whatever is necessary for your child to come into the world." At the conclusion, she seemed a little perplexed and said, "But it's not giving an *ebo* to perform. You should have to get blessings from the women in your family for this type of divination, but it's not saying anything here."

Upon her utterance of those last words, I knew my trip home had been the ebo or *sacrifice* that Iya Sangode was looking for. It seemed to ease her mind when I told her about my hometown visit. A very experienced and skilled diviner, the confirmation let me know that Iya Sangode's reading was what it should have been under the circumstances.

To avoid the declines indicated previously by Malidoma Somé, and possible child birth issues like I had, we must consider that the time of adolescence and entering the young adult phase of life can be both exciting and disconcerting. The youth themselves realize that something "different" is happening to them, i.e., hormones are raging, girls' bodies begin to swell in certain areas, pubic hairs are appearing in both sexes, and facial hairs start to transform boyish looks into handsome features. Girls experience the magical phenomenon that allows them to add to the population of the planet -- menstruation. And, with a little assistance from curious teen-age guys, they are more often than not, willing to *try it out*. But with the contemporary onset of deadly sexually transmitted diseases, abortions, high divorce rates and the rising number of single parent households, teens really should think seriously before engaging in sex. This is why it is important to *catch* the youth at the onset of puberty, a critical time in their lives, so that certain things can be explained (in a meaningful way) and implanted in their conscious and subconscious mind.

In Native American and in the Yoruba culture of West Africa (Nigeria) as well as in the United States and certain Caribbean islands, like other cultures in West Africa (Dagara, Akan, etc.), the importance of this time is not simply highlighted with a big party that lasts only a few hours. Rather, there is often a lot of preparation for the ceremonies. Among the Apache and Navajo, elders, priests and the whole community/village may become participants in a process that begins around age 12 (or at the first *menarchie* (menstrual period), also called *kinaalda*. It can continue throughout the teenage years until the child is no longer an adolescent but, a young adult. More importantly, the rituals that are performed are so strikingly different from every day occurrences that the experience is forever engrained in the mind and memory of the youth, leaving an indelible mark on their existence in the human family.

Humility

We must remember to have a sense of humility when performing ceremonies, such as rites of passage. When requesting spiritual help, in essence *divine intervention*, we must not think that we can simply command spirit to do our will (although there are times when we come close).

Invocation is the request of a person to the spirit of God for divine intervention. Somé relates that "*The language of invocation must not be confused with order and command. It must be closer to a plea, a humble request. This is because ritual is a spirit-based activity performed by humans. For anything to happen, the ritual must be dominated by humility.*" Christians will relate to this aspect of ritual from an old hymn, "*Pass me not, oh gentle Saviour. Hear my humble cry. Whilst on others thou art calling, do not pass me by.*"

Sometimes a song says it all. Drumming and singing were always integral components of ritual in indigenous societies. Indicative of the heart beat and the continuous rhythm of life and how everything is intertwined, for the most part, you did not have ritual without the drum and song. While in churches, the drumming has been replaced by the piano or organ, and in some cases, by an entire band or small orchestra, the practice is still rooted in ancient customs.

Still it is the sense of humility that must permeate transition rituals. When invoking the presence of a power greater than ourselves -- the Great Mystery, to bless our children, it is my experience that one feels compelled to be humble before the awesomeness of God. Truly, to bring children into the world today I believe, we must trust in that supreme being for guidance on their life paths.

What is Culture?

Culture is the practices and customs indicative of a certain group of people and their way of life. It does not define a people, rather, it shapes their lives and gives insight into their ways and beliefs, as well as lays a foundation for who they are.

The Culture of the American

When you look at their ancestral lineage, their common heritage with other ethnic groups and fate of history, the American is arguably the most *cultured* group in the world. On one hand, the descendants of Africans whose fore-parents came via forced migration to North American shores, for the most part stemmed from various ethnic societies and nations along the west coast of Africa. Their languages were similar but different. Europeans may have started coming from Spain initially, but they were soon joined by others from France, the British Isles, Germany, Scandinavia and various Slavic and Baltic states. Their customs were similar but different. The religions of theAfricans were either *rainforest type* systems of worship wherein they worshipped forces of nature *and* a supreme being, or they practiced Islam, or various forms of Christianity, like the Europeans. Islam and Christianity were foreign importations.

Religion

Defined as "a set of beliefs concerning the cause, nature, and purpose of the universe, especially belief in the worship of God or Gods," *religion* is a system in which a group of people or individuals practice the worship of God or some other force they deem greater than themselves.

Most prominent among world religions however, are Christianity, Islam, Judaism, Buddhism. Of course, under all of these are varying denominations. Under Christianity we have Protestants, Catholics, Armenian, Ethiopian Oriental Orthodox, Baptists, AME, Wesleyan, Pentecostal, etc. Under Islam in the east we have Islamic Fundamentalists, Shiites, Suni, Orthodox and a whole plethora of other Islamic bands. In the west are the Nation of Islam, as well as Moorish Science Temple Moslems, Suni and Orthodox muslims -- among others. In Judaism there are Orthodox Jews, Hebrew Israelites, Israelis, Sephardim (decendants of Spanish and Portuguese Jews), Ashkenazim (descendants of Jews who settled in north and central Europe, (particularly Germany), and even Jews for Jesus, etc. Africa boasts of many diverse shamanistic-type religious practices, including that of the Bushmen of Kalahari. The same goes for the Pacific southwest where we have the Sambia of New Guinea and in the north are the Eskimo [Inuit] of Alaska (U.S.) and Newfoundland (Canada). In South America Peru is home to the Mestizos (what used to be a term for Mexicans of mixed European and American Indian heritage and now called *vegetalista* because of their use of strong herbs for healing).

COMBINING CULTURE WITH SPIRITUALITY

In this take on rites of passage, it does not matter what religion you practice. You simply use the basis of your culture and your religion as a foundation for preparing children to go out into the world as *divine human beings.*

The key is impressing upon them the understanding that, in the perfection of God, the child was made *a divine human being and placed in the world among other like beings.* Yes, as they grow they are taught to be anything but divine because of various influences in society -- lying, cheating, stealing, fighting, warring, coveting others' possessions, other mates. But, understand -- these are learned behaviors. We come into the world divine. A newborn baby is as perfect and divine as a ray of sun, or snow falling silently from the sky. When the baby wraps its entire little hand around your finger for the very first time, no one has to tell you what a precious act that is.

While we are all going to engage in some less than divine behaviors and activities, being the imperfect beings that we are, in rites of passage we try to impress upon the candidates the importance of recognizing their divinity, because, when they see divinity in themselves, they can see it in others. This is a basis for how they will treat humanity as they walk their life's journey. If the adage is true that "You get what you give," then their goodwill, their love and their trust in humanity will in the long run reap them rewards of the same.

Oyotunji African Village

Oyotunji African Village, located in Beaufort County, South Carolina (approx. 55 miles south of Charleston), was founded by Oba Oseijeman Adefunmi and a handful of Yoruba priests and priestesses in the early 1970s. A contemporary of Martin

Luther King, Jr., Adefunmi became a pioneer in the study and promulgation of Yoruba culture. His intent was the establishment of an authentic African village in America where residents could essentially live, eat and drink African religion in an afrocentric environment.

Isolated and away from the everyday intrusions of western living, at one time Oyotunji had as many as 300 families living within its gates. In a twelve acre setting, similar to that of a monastery, worship of Yoruba gods and goddesses were their focus.

Recognizing that historically, many African Americans had cultural roots in west Africa, Adefunmi followed a path to Yoruba culture. His study and initiations led him to the conclusion that reclamation of the religion of their ancestors was paramount to the spiritual development of African Americans. In that regard, he comments:

> "It is a profound "cultural void" which reduces the African American imagination to impotence when situations and conditions, either favorable or unfavorable, suddenly occur. It is lack of a refined frame of reference which prevents wise choices and decisions in moments germane to racial advancement or survival. It is the loss of cultural hindsight which induces the evaporation of any self-willed vision of the future. This "cultural amnesia" is the greatest abomination which can befall an individual, a generation, or a nation, since the human quality of each individual, each generation, and in time the entire people, progressively decline...."

The above statement indicates a continuity in thinking by some continental Africans (such as Somé), African Americans who live an African-based cultural lifestyle, and other indigenous clerics. The naming of African American children with names that are unmistakably intended to make a connection to African roots further demonstrates this continuity. The idea that there will be a decline in generations if certain cultural practices germane to their existence are overlooked and not observed is clear.

In any case, the religious persuasions of African Americans greatly influenced their cultural practices, sufficiently enough to conclude that the blending of culture with their religion resulted in these people being of an intensely spiritual and religious nature. Likewise, those who are descended from unions with Native Americans are similarly pre-supposed to be highly spiritual.

This is probably not the case for *atheists*.

But, it is likely that any group of people who experience great trauma heaped upon them *because* of their cultural or religious backgrounds, tend to be spiritually inclined because they generally believe a higher power is responsible for their survival. In another discussion, the same could hold true for groups of people from varying backgrounds who experience a great tragedy, a terrorist situation or natural catastrophe together. Even many criminals or non-criminals who find themselves incarcerated due to their own actions or unjust legal verdicts tend to "get religion" or they believe their lives *on the inside* are sustained by God when they have lengthy or even death sentences.

RITUALS

In *Ritual - Power, Healing and Community*, Malidoma Patrice Somé defines ceremony as *the structure of ritual*. He explains that *"the invisible part of the ritual, that which actually happens as a result of the ceremony, is what carries the ritual quality within itself."*

When the youth is ready to be presented as one who is prepared to go through a rites of passage process, an elder or medicine/spiritual person (facilitator) who understands *the structure of ritual* should be contacted (if one does not or has not already presented herself to you (think about it -- perhaps they have). Upon notification of this, the facilitator will *utilize her own traditions from which she will perform the ceremony, along with traditions familiar to the candidate.* In this regard, she may use ancient customs but will couple them with the candidate's current spiritual inclination.

An Involved Process

For instance, the facilitator must pray for guidance and ask what she should do specifically for the youth being presented. If there is more than one candidate (a group) for the rites of passage, the facilitator must ask for guidance regarding what is to be done for *each individual candidate* because no two individuals are exactly alike and, they may not need the exact same thing. Of course, depending on the facilitator's spiritual or religious persuasion, the spiritual consultation will vary. In any case, if we are familiar with the phrase, *pray on it*, this is the time for the facilitator to do just that. If we want to get it right, we better *pray on it*.

If we don't know how to pray then we should consider that perhaps we are not ready to perform this kind of ceremony.

A Yoruba priest would consult the *Ifa oracle*, a system of divination, using cowrie shells or kola nuts and the complex interpretations of what the oracle reveals. Afterwards, there may be a number of *ebos* to be performed. These are things the candidate must do in order to remedy an existing situation or one that may arise which could impact the candidate's destiny.

Native Americans who perform rites of passage ceremonies away from reservations may have to improvise a little more and may utilize a number of practices. The medicine person may pray after smoking a *chanunpa* or *pipe* filled with *ki-nic-nic* or some other natural, non-narcotic herb, or, if she has a place out in the countryside, she might have a sweat lodge ceremony to gain the needed guidance and clarity. The use of the pipe is explained in the Lakota legend about the White Buffalo Woman.

A Christian minister might simply pray or *fast* and pray. Whatever the means, this is a most important first step in the ritual which, as we can see, is not simply a one-day event. Rather, *the ritual is a series of tasks performed by the candidate and the facilitator and persons closely related to the candidate, who will have an integral part in the candidate's growth and development*. Rites of passage can be an extremely involved process.

In any event, once the actual ceremony is being performed, if the facilitator is well versed in any particular spiritual or religious tradition she should use methods which will work well in the setting before her. She must also ask/pray for guidance as to the spiritual tradition of the candidate. In this regard, the facilitator may be guided to utilize references, doctrine or items familiar to the candidate. There is a two-fold purpose to this spiritual consultation. It prevents the candidate from being spooked, and it makes her more at ease and thus, more accepting of whatever message is revealed to her through this process.

Once the facilitator has *divined* or prayed on the matter at hand -- the ritual structure, she should meet with the candidate and her parents (particularly her mother) to counsel them about the ritual and what they must do to prepare for it. It should be impressed upon them that taking this step is not a frivolous act, rather, it indicates the parents' willingness to give to children something important that they perhaps did not have.

While the parents may have had an informal type of initiation, if they were unaware of it and never gained a real understanding of it, then its impact would obviously have fallen short, as is the case with some parents whose upbringing was in a rural, agrarian setting. Learning to live from the land and interacting with farm animals (or animals in the wild) can be a *roots inspired* (very basic) lifestyle wherein an appreciation of the complexities yet simplicity of life is taught and learned. Modern conveniences, like mega supermarkets, convenience stores and department stores, may allow more time for other activities but they also infringe upon the quiet time that people have who live from the earth without those conveniences. The solitude of farming/gardening, herding, spinning thread into cloth, sewing out of necessity, curing and smoking one's own meats, etc., was and is hard work but its reward is attaining the ability to survive from the land and be content within one's knowing of the workings of spirit. Why? Because one is forced to trust it more.

The candidate and her parents will have to be encouraged to *quiet their minds* during this time as much as possible. This is in order to *hear* the lessons to be derived from the process. When one is constantly bombarded with work, arguments, and concerns of others that are totally unrelated to anything spiritual it is easy to take the process for granted. However, one must not lose sight that the facilitator is only a connector -- a conduit being utilized for the implementation of the rites of passage initiation. One must yield to the fact that the ultimate success or failure of the ritual is on one and one's family. Their hearts and minds must be clear and free from thoughts of ill-will, negativity and selfishness. The parents have called on God to help their children and they must now show the humility they should have when prostrating before the omnipotence of The Great Spirit and the ancestral angels who are now availing themselves.

The Story of the White Buffalo Calf (Pipe) Woman

An adage of the Sioux is that "Woman shall not walk before man." But, the White Buffalo Woman is central to the history of their very survival. Explained by Crow Dog, a renowned Sioux medicine man, he stated "This holy woman brought the sacred buffalo calf pipe to the Sioux. There could be no Indians without it. Before she came, people didn't know how to live. They knew nothing. The Buffalo Woman put her sacred mind into their minds." Her sacred standing among the Sioux is also exemplified at their Sun Dance rituals where one woman, a mature and well-respected member of the tribe, is given the opportunity of performing the role of the Buffalo Woman.

First appearing to the Sioux as a human, White Buffalo Woman also appeared as a buffalo. In reading the following legend, one understands why the white buffalo is so sacred to the Plains tribes, and a white buffalo hide a priceless possession.

****

One summer so long ago that nobody knows how long, the *Oceti-Shakowi*, the seven sacred council fires of the Lakota *Oyate*, the nation, came together and camped. The sun shone all the time, but there was no game and the people were starving. Every day they sent scouts to look for game, but the scouts found nothing.

Among the bands assembled were the *Itazipcho*, the Without-Bows, who had their own camp circle under their chief, Standing Hollow Horn. Early one morning the chief sent two of his young men to hunt for game. They went on foot, because at that time the Sioux did not yet have horses. They searched everywhere but could find nothing. Seeing a high hill, they decided to climb it in order to look over the whole country.

Halfway up, they saw something coming toward them from far off, but the figure was floating instead of walking. From this they knew that the person was *wakan*, holy.

At first they could make out only a small moving speck and had to squint to see that it was a human form. But as it came nearer, they realized that it was a beautiful young woman, more beautiful than any they had ever seen, with two round, red dots of face paint on her cheeks. She wore a wonderful white buckskin outfit, tanned until it shone a long way in the sun. It was embroidered with sacred and marvelous designs of porcupine quill, in radiant colors no ordinary woman could have made. This *wakan* stranger was *Ptesan-Wi*, White Buffalo Woman. In her hands she carried a large bundle and a fan of sage leaves. She wore her blue-black hair loose except for a strand at the left side, which was tied up with buffalo fur. Her eyes shone dark and sparkling, with great power in them.

The two young men looked at her open-mouthed. One was overawed, but the other desired her body and stretched his hand out to touch her. This woman was *lila wakan*, very sacred, and could not be treated with disrespect. Lightning instantly struck the brash young man and burned him up, so that only a small heap of blackened bones was left. Some say that he was suddenly covered by a cloud and within it he was eaten up by snakes that left only his bones, just as a man can be eaten up by lust.

To the other scout who had behaved rightly, the White Buffalo Woman said: "Good things I am bringing, something holy to your nation. A message I carry for your people from the buffalo nation. Go back to the camp and tell the people to prepare for my arrival. Tell your chief to put up a medicine lodge with twenty-four poles. Let it be made holy for my coming."

This young hunter returned to the camp. He told the chief and the people what the sacred woman had commanded.

The chief told the *eyapah*, the crier, and the crier went through the camp circle calling: "Someone sacred is coming. A holy woman approaches. Make all things ready for her." So the people put up the big medicine tipi and waited. After four days they saw the White Buffalo Woman approaching, carrying her bundle before her. Her wonderful white buckskin dress shone from afar. The chief, Standing Hollow Horn, invited her to enter the medicine lodge. She went in and circled the interior sunwise. The chief addressed her respectfully, saying: "Sister, we are glad you have come to instruct us."

She told him what she wanted done. In the center of the tipi they were to put up an *owanka wakan*, a sacred altar, made of red earth, with a buffalo skull and a three-stick rack for a holy thing she was bringing. They did what she directed, and she traced a design with her finger on the smoothed earth of the altar. She showed them how to do all this, then circled the lodge again sunwise. Halting before the chief, she now opened the bundle. The holy thing it contained was the *chanunpa*, the sacred pipe. She held it out to the people and let them look at it. She was grasping the stem with her right hand and the bowl with her left, and thus the pipe has been held ever since.

Again, the chief spoke, saying: "Sister, we are glad. We have had no meat for some time. All we can give you is water." They dipped some *wacanga*, sweet grass, into a skin bag of water and gave it to her, and to this day the people dip sweet grass or an eagle wing in water and sprinkle it on a person to be purified.

The White Buffalo Woman showed the people how to use the pipe. She filled it with *chan-shasha*, red willow bark tobacco. She walked around the lodge four times after the manner of Anpetu-Wi, the great sun. This represented the circle without end, the sacred hoop, the road of life. The woman placed a dry buffalo chip on the fire and lit the pipe with it. This was *peta-owihankeshni*, the fire without end, the flame to be passed on from generation to generation. She told them that the smoke rising from the bowl was Tunkashila's breath, the living breath of the great Grandfather Mystery.

The White Buffalo Woman showed the people the right way to pray, the right words and the right gestures. She taught them how to sing the pipe-filling song and how to lift the pipe up to the sky, toward Grandfather, and down toward Grandmother Earth, to Unci, and then to the four directions of the universe.

"With this holy pipe," she said, "you will walk like a living prayer. With your feet resting upon the earth and the pipestem reaching into the sky, your body forms a living bridge between the Sacred Beneath and the Sacred Above. Wakan Tanka smiles upon us, because now we are as one: earth, sky, all living things, the two-legged, the four-legged, the winged ones, the trees, the grasses. Together with the people, they are all related, one family. The pipe holds them all together.

"Look at this bowl," said the White Buffalo Woman. "Its stone represents the buffalo, but also the flesh and blood of the red man. The buffalo represents the universe and the four directions, because he stands on four legs, for the four ages of creation. The buffalo was put in the west by *Wakan Tanka* at the making of the world, to hold back the waters. Every year he loses one hair, and in every one of the four ages he loses a leg. The sacred hoop will end when all the hair and legs of the great buffalo are gone, and the water comes back to cover the Earth.

The wooden stem of this *chanunpa* stands for all that grows on the earth. Twelve feathers hanging from where the stem -- the backbone -- joins the bowl -- the skull -- are from *Wanblee Galeshka*, the spotted eagle, the very sacred bird who is the Great Spirit's messenger and the wisest of all flying ones. You are joined to all things of the universe, for they all cry out to *Tunkashila*. Look at the bowl: engraved in it are seven circles of various sizes. They stand for the seven sacred ceremonies you will practice with this pipe, and for the *Ocheti Shakowin*, the seven sacred campfires of our Lakota nation."

The White Buffalo Woman then spoke to the women, telling them that it was the work of their hands and the fruit of their bodies which kept the people alive. "You are from the mother earth," she told them. "What you are doing is as great as what the warriors do."

And therefore the sacred pipe is also something that binds men and women together in a circle of love. It is the only holy object in the making of which both men and women have a hand. The men carve the bowl and make the stem; the women decorate it with bands of colored porcupine quills. When a man takes a wife, they both hold the pipe at the same time and red trade cloth is wound around their hands, thus tying them together for life.

The White Buffalo Woman had many things for her Lakota sisters in her sacred womb bag -- corn, *wasna* (pemmican), wild turnip. She taught them how to make the hearth fire. She filled a buffalo paunch with cold water and dropped a red-hot stone into it. "This way you shall cook the corn and the meat," she told them

The White Buffalo Woman also talked to the children, because they have an understanding beyond their years. She told them that what their fathers and mothers did was for them, that their parents could remember being little once, and that they, the children, would grow up to have little ones of their own. She told them: "You are the coming generation, that's why you are the most important and precious ones. Some day you will hold this pipe and smoke it. Some day you will pray with it."

She spoke once more to all the people: The pipe is alive; it is a red being showing you a red life and a red road. And this is the first ceremony for which you will use the pipe. You will use it to keep the soul of a dead person, because through it you can talk to Wakan Tanka, the Great Mystery Spirit. The day a human dies is always a sacred day. The day when the soul is released to the Great Spirit is another. *Four* women will become sacred on such a day. They will be the ones to cut the sacred tree -- the *can-wakan* -- for the sun dance."

She told the Lakota that they were the purest among the tribes, and for that reason Tunkashila had bestowed upon them the holy *chanunpa*. They had been chosen to take care of it for all the Indian people on this turtle continent.

She spoke one last time to Standing Hollow Horn, the chief, saying, "Remember: this pipe is very sacred. Respect it and it will take you to the end of the road. The four ages of creation are in me; I am the four ages. I will come to see you in every generation cycle. I shall come back to you."

The sacred woman then took leave of the people saying: "*Toksha ake wacinyanktin ktelo* -- I shall see you again." The people saw her walking off in the same direction from which she had come, outlined against the red ball of the setting sun. As she went, she stopped and rolled over four times. The first time, she turned into a black buffalo; the second into a brown one; the third into a red one; and finally, the fourth time she rolled over, she turned into a white female buffalo calf. A white buffalo is the most sacred living thing you could ever encounter.

The White Buffalo Woman disappeared over the horizon. Sometime she might come back. As soon as she had vanished, buffalo in great herds appeared, allowing themselves to be killed so that the people might survive. And from that day on, our relations, the buffalo, furnished the people with everything they needed -- meat for their food, skins for their clothes and tipis, bones for their many tools.

--This account was told by John Fire Lame Deer at Winner, Rosebud Indian Reservation, South Dakota, 1967.

Vision Quest

If a *vision quest* is prescribed, this is generally a more time-consuming tool in a rites of passage.

Among the Plateau groups of native people, vision quests were done by both boys and girls coming into puberty, but in some tribes it is only the young males who *seek their vision*. When performed by a female, puberty is the only time she would go on a vision quest, but for the male, puberty may only be one of possibly many vision quests throughout his life.

In itself a rite of passage, a vision quest is where the candidate spends days in isolation in the wilderness, communing with nature, residing with the animals of the desert or the forest, and using the Earth Mother for a bed and the moon and stars as a canopy. Surviving only on water and whatever one can find for sustenance has a way of bringing one to a spiritual awakening. In the Lakota tradition, young men facing manhood would go on a vision quest to ask for a vision of what was asked of their lives.

Humblecheyasi is the term used for the vision quest, which means "crying for a vision." This quest was also undertaken by women and older men.

There is also such a thing which I call an *urban vision quest*. It takes place in a city or an urban environment, but the candidate experiences isolation for several days and totally exists at the direction of and to a large extent, under the control of the medicine person, who provides guidance and sustenance. Perhaps she is not *in* the *wilderness* but she feels like she is because there is no contact with other people, no telephone, no television or radio. She may be given spiritual baths, and made to sit or lay prostrate for lengthy periods of time in complete meditation. This can be a most enlightening and soul-searching experience.

Sweat Lodge

The *sweat lodge* is a ceremonial earthen prayer house constructed of long cylindrical tree branches bent over, bound together and covered with animal hides and/or thick leaves (or heavy cloth in some cases) and can be compared superficially to a sauna. But their use goes far beyond simply working up a good sweat. Traditional lodges are done separately for the sexes, i.e., men sweat together, women sweat together and children sweat together but with adult supervision. Once the lodge is built, further preparation entails gathering a lot of big rocks between the size of a large grapefruit and a large honeydew melon. A bonfire is started on the ground close to the lodge for heating the rocks.

A *fire tender* is appointed to manage the fire and to supply the lodge with the rocks when called for by the person leading the lodge (a *carrier of the lodge*). The rocks must be heated to soaring temperatures which cause them to become fire red, almost transparent. Though the person tending the fire does not go into the lodge, her responsibility of heating the rocks is key to a good sweat lodge, which makes his/her presence and his/her job particularly important. He/she must be spiritually in tune and physically fit for the task. Physical strength is necessary to lift the rocks from the fire with a heavy pitch fork or shovel and place them into the central pit of the lodge. Thus, any injury to lodge participants can be prevented. The fire tender must also be careful that the fire is not too close to the lodge as a further precaution.

Once the central pit is filled with scorching hot rocks, which are doused with water and herbs like small pieces of sweetgrass and cedar, the sinuses are opened and the head becomes clear, but to say that this is all there is to it -- is a gross understatement. Fervent singing, praying and a deafening silence while sitting in total darkness certainly brings the participant to a spiritual experience unlike any other.

*Note: Today, although considered a *New Age* activity, across the United States, *communal (co-ed)* sweat lodges are hosted by a variety of people. Sometimes the lodge "carrier" is a non-Native person who has received some training from a Native American medicine man/woman or, one who has simply obtained some information about the history of the sweat lodge and host gatherings to share information. Others try to help those who may be suffering from an illness to purify themselves. If someone has an obvious illness he should not enter a sweat lodge with others for fear of passing on the illness. Still for some, it is simply a social gathering. None of the aforementioned diminishes the sacredness of the sweat lodge and its role in certain rituals.

APACHE AND NAVAJO TRADITIONS

Among many Native American tribes, when a young girl had her first menstruation it was seen as a joyous occasion and one of solemn promise. Because she was now becoming imbued with the strength of the female, the young teen or pre-teen girl was, for the most part, isolated and only allowed to come in contact with other women. It was believed that females were too powerful during their menstruation period to be out in the villages as their blood flow might affect the outcome of wars and hunting -- both of which greatly impacted the survival of the village.

For the Apache, the *White Painted Woman* survived an enormous flood to become the first of all humans, unlike the biblical Genesis account wherein Adam -- a man, was the first human. For the Navajo, it was *Changing Woman* (Esdzaanadleehe), a Holy Person instrumental in the tribe's creation, who had the first *kinaalda* (menstrual period). The legend is that the Holy People sang her into a new level of her life. These rites of passage ceremonies last four days but there is at least a month of preparation to bring the budding pubescent girl into womanhood. Her fertility is celebrated with dancing and body painting, feasting, and she is seen as the incarnate Changing Woman or White Painted Woman during that time.

The Apache commence their four days with a *Sunrise Ceremony*. During this time the young woman is said to take on the healing powers of White Painted Woman, signifying a critical moment in her young history. Each day she must run to the four directions of her village at sunrise and the attendants who are participating and facilitating the rites of passage must also run with her. The elder medicine woman sings special songs for her and she is blessed with sacred cattail pollen by villagers as she passes through, and they in turn ask her blessing upon them, as she has been imbued with healing powers. At night, the Ga'an or Crown Dancers, believed to be powerful protector spirits of the Apache, come down from their

mountain homelands and dance with the candidate. Much like the
Gelede Dancers or Egun-gun of the Yoruba, masked dancers arrive
to lively drumming, bells ringing, chanting or singing, and they
are adorned in elaborate and sometimes fierce-looking, brightly
colored costumes. The intense energy they exhibit and generate
among the villagers alone indicates the awesome nature and largess
of the power of the protector spirit or ancestral spirit, which has
materialized on the earthly plane to commune with the candidate
and villagers. The air is charged with contagious excitement and
it is an impressive site to witness -- a fitting beginning to the
ceremony as anticipation mounts during the preparation time and
as the days begin to unfold.

On the fourth day of the Apache ritual, the candidate is painted
with white clay -- symbols of the White Painted Woman are
reproduced all over her body. Her attendants, facilitators and
guests join in a dance procession behind her as the holy people sing
or chant a song that signifies she is now *a woman.* The vibration
is such that it's as though the Earth Mother herself hallows the
ground as she gives her blessing upon one of her daughters.

GHOST DANCE

Historically, the story of the Ghost Dance came to prominence through accounts of the massacre of a group of Sioux Indians in December 1890. I refer to the *wanagi-wachipi* (Ghost Dance *religion* as American historians have called it), merely to relate its practice to the topic herein -- rites of passage. While it was not a puberty or fertility dance, it nevertheless could be regarded as a rite of passage tradition because it was in preparation for the Native people's transition from a time of misery and conquest to a new millennium which was believed would usher in an era of peace, happiness and security.

When talking about the candidate arriving at a sacred place within herself, I am reminded of the many Native American tribes or nations of people who once practiced the Ghost Dance. It was revealed to them through a Paiute man called Wovaka The Messiah.

Born circa 1856 of his mother and his father Taribo, Wovoka was said to be born with the gift of sight -- capable of having visions and seeing what would come in the future. Wovoka's father, who was himself considered a prophet by his people, had a great influence on him. When Taribo passed away, Wovoka, who was only fourteen years old at the time, began to have more visions and they became increasingly clear and powerful. Ultimately, he would go into a deep trance and in that state, he received a revelation of a dance which he was to share with the native people. Wokova said that the people were to ..."Do no harm to anyone. Do right always..." This was possibly in response to growing tensions among the native people and the settlers because the whites had taken over the land, leaving the native people on reservations and in extremely restricted conditions.

The Ghost Dance was based on the underlying premise that "The time will come when the [Indian] race, living and dead, will be regenerated upon a regenerated earth, to live in a life of aboriginal happiness forever, free from death, disease and misery... Whites, being alien and *hardly real*, will have no part in this aboriginal regeneration, ... and will be left with other things of the earth that have served their temporary purpose, or else will cease entirely to exist."

It is an overriding spiritual power that is to bring about the fulfillment of the prophecy. The time projected was at the advent of the [Indian] millennium and it would occur in the spring, or to be more exact, around the fourth of July. This is the time when the annual Ghost Dance ceremonies take place among the Sioux in the east, and the Apache, Kiowa, Cheyenne, Arapaho, Caddo, Ute and Paiute in the west. Medicine men (*wichasha wakan*) were supposed to be able to anticipate the exact time of the change.

Among the Paiute, the Ghost Dance was performed around a central tree or pole. Fires were built within or near the circle, but, the prairie tribes forbade fire within the circle. Outside of the ring there were normally some structures built from tree branches, in some cases, willow bark, where Wokova would go into a trance and while under, he would tell the people about the spirit world. The dance would be performed for four days and possibly the morning of the fifth and final day.

At the onset of the Wounded Knee tragedy, the Sioux had become disgruntled with the government's handling of their people and their land. Turning to their faith was their only consolation. Unfortunately for them, however, in the midst of their trance the Ghost Dancers were attacked by white soldiers.

Ignorant to the ceremony and with the federal government having made it illegal for [Indians] to practice their own religious traditions, when the fur-clad soldiers ordered the Sioux to stop dancing, the soldiers took their unresponsiveness (due to their being in a state of trance) to be an act of sheer defiance and abruptly opened fire, killing some men, but mostly women and children. It was in the dead of winter, and many froze where they fell. Their contorted, partially snow-covered bodies were found still expressing the horror of murdered defenseless people by attackers who saw no value in (Indian) lives.

In a twisted historical precursor to the Jewish holocaust and over 200 years after the first shipload of kidnapped Africans were brought to the shores of Turtle Island, the American soldiers stacked the dead bodies like firewood. Dick Fool Bull saw a dead mother with her deceased baby sucking at her breast, and he lived to tell the tale. The child wore a beaded cap with the design of the American Flag.

Sadly, while it did not lead them to the transition time in the manner in which the Sioux at Wounded Knee Creek thought it would come, they nevertheless were sent to the spirit world through their practice of the Ghost Dance. We can only hope that once they made their transition, it was as beautiful for them as their messiah Wokova had predicted.

During the time of the Wounded Knee (*Chankpe-op Wakpala)* uprising in 1973, Indian civil rights activists had a 73-day stand-off with U.S. Marshalls and the FBI at the site of the 1890 massacre. Native Americans were still protesting their treatment which historically stemmed from their being moved around, due to illegal land grants to settlers and the federal government's constant reneging on agreements regarding Native American lands. When the protest was finally put down by the federal government, two Indians were killed, one of whom was buried next to one of his ancestors who had met the same fate in the massacre of 1890.

This is a significant piece of history to share with young people. As they go through their rites of passage they need to know to what lengths people have gone to in the past to suppress these kinds of rituals, and that some of our ancestors sacrificed their very lives so that we could live to enjoy the freedom we have to honor them and to worship God in our own unique way.

The [American] Religious Crimes Code banned all forms of Native American spiritual practices, including consulting medicine persons, praying to God in their own methods, language, and ceremonial dances. In the same manner that the Jesuit religious order tried to *program* the Dagara children who they kidnapped from Malidoma Somé's village in Africa, and forbade them from worshiping in their own way, the Sioux along with other Native American tribes were taught to be ashamed of their ancestors, their language and their heritage.

The irony is that the government of a nation founded upon the promise of liberties denied them in Europe, specifically religious freedom, deemed it necessary and indeed *acceptable* to outlaw Native American spiritual practices in order to advance a thorough take-over of the land and decimation and destruction of native culture, religion and lifestyle, and the very thought processes of the indigenous.

The question that should be asked then, why was it so important to stop Native people from worshipping God in their own way, in their own tongue, and practicing their traditional customs. The answer undoubtedly is that in order to conquer a people, you must break their spirit. To truly control them you must take away their concept of God and replace it with something else. When you take away a people's perception of God and their ability to see God in them, you in fact *remove* God in them. That is what was attempted with Native and African people the world over. Many others (Jews, Palestinians, Irish, Serbians, on and on) have been victims of persecution. Now is the time however to reclaim our spirit through a process of recreating our own cultural traditions and performing our rituals.

People have always been defined by their customs and spiritual practices. Still today, though the distinctions have become grayed in light of musical cross-overs and more inter-denominational and multi-racial church congregations, there is yet a difference in how Native/aboriginal people worship and their euro-centric counterparts. In general, Afro-centric religious services tend to be more lively, and, in some cases, more *entertaining* than eurocentric religious services. These distinctions are not bad or wrong. They just are. People are products not only of their present environment, but of their past spiritually connected environment as well. It makes us who we are. Yes, there was genocide but not gene-o-cide. The genes have been passed down and that which responds to the sweet breath of the Earth Mother, her heartbeat and the thunder and lightning of the Father God is alive and well in us. We must simply rekindle our relationship.

For a healing to take place, the source of the pain or dis-ease must be identified, then the cause of the discomfort has to be acknowledged. If native people suffer today because their customs and rituals were stripped from them and their function ceased, we must acknowledge that truth. The remedy then is to either resurrect the ancient rituals or to pray for guidance to develop new methods.

This is where we are in our spiritual development – coming full circle – from knowing to not knowing – to knowing a little something then not knowing anything – to finding ourselves again and re-connecting with our spirit.

THE YORUBA TRADITION

Girls' and young women's training in the *Egbe Obinrin* (Society of Women) at Oyotunji African Village in South Carolina will go on for several years, first through pre-adolescence and into the young adult years. It consists of a training regimen geared towards building strength in women, protection of and emancipation of women, nurturing and guidance of babies and young children, and enhancing the welfare and development of the community. Girls are trained not only to be women, but to be mothers and sisters to other women. There are classes that they must attend that vary from cooking and sewing to child care, music, dance, calisthenics, self-defense, etiquette and hygiene. African and Women's history are taught, as well as marriage and relationships.

At the end of the training period, usually a group of young women will participate in a *going over* or rites of passage ceremony, marking their graduation. The girls engage in a ritual bath, whitening of their bodies with efun (chalk), followed by the taking of an oath, recitation of a pledge, and then receiving Egbe marks on their arms. They are thereafter presented to the public during the Women's Festival, which is normally during the celebration of Yemoja, the mother goddess of the Yoruba. Upon completion of their training, the women are full fledged members in the Egbe Moremi society.

The Story of Moremi

Egbe Moremi is the Society (Egbe) of women under the sponsorship of the great Queen of Ife, Moremi. The story of Moremi is that at the time that Moremi was a queen of Ife, her town was constantly being attacked by invaders dressed in costumes. Moremi allowed herself to be captured on one of these raids. As she was very beautiful, Moremi was given to the king of the invading tribe. As time passed, the king became enamored with her and told her of the secret of the invaders. Moremi slipped away and returned to Ife and shared the secret.

The next time the invaders came, the people of Ife were ready. They set fire to the invaders' costumes and the invaders retreated in defeat. But Moremi had made a pact with the deity of the river. In exchange for Moremi saving Ife, she had to sacrifice her only son to the spirit of the river. All the town mourned for Moremi and pledged that their children would be her own.

Moremi's story so inspired the women of Oyotunji African Village that she became the patron of the Society of Women-Egbe Moremi.

www.oyotunjivillage.net

The Ultimate Rite of Passage and Egungun

In the Yoruba culture, death is a transition time which is considered a form of graduation into a higher existence where the spirit receives new enlightenment before returning to his/her family as a new baby. Thus, in order for a good family spirit not to be lost in the spirit world, and so that it may use its out-of-body powers to aid those left behind, the Yoruba, like Africans throughout the diaspora, venerate the spirits of their ancestors with regular offerings of food, prayers, parties and ceremonies.

When a person dies and is buried after three days, a second funeral is held for his/her *ghost* eight days later. This ghost is someone who has been dressed up to look like the dead man or woman, and who becomes possessed by the spirit of the dead person. This person in his/her elaborate costume, becomes the *Egungun*. The [3]Egungun

---

[3] The *Egungun Society* generally consists of members of a village or area in the Yoruba culture, who are prone to be profoundly affected by spirits and are often those who may become possessed, perhaps more readily in ceremonial settings. In light of this, they are likely choices to take on the personage of a deceased member of their community for the final rites. Egungun Society members are distinguished in ancestral processions and parades by colorful multi-ribboned or multi-colored skirts and ceremonial beads that they wear, indicating their initiation into the Egungun Society.

Society then escorts the Egungun from a grove in the forest to the place where its descendants live, where it is met by its living family. Final wishes, farewells and blessings are exchanged. Gifts and food are served to the drummers and singers who escort the Egungun throughout the village. When they have departed, a second funeral celebration is held with much dancing, speech making and music to honor the dead.

THE KROBO AND ASHANTI

The *Krobo* and Ashanti are two groups in Ghana with well-founded traditions in rites of passage and notably, *nubility* rites which refer to rituals performed for those "ready for marriage" or being of the marrying age.

Interestingly, many African Americans who have been able to trace their heritage have found that some of their ancestors came from the coasts of Senegal and Ghana in Africa. If kidnapped during the time of the Middle Passage, they may very well have participated in the ceremonies of the Krobo and the Ashanti before passing through the infamous "door of no return" at Gorée Isle, where it is reported that upwards of 60,000 captured Africans were held as *merchandise* for slave traders. Some African American groups which conduct rites of passage ceremonies sponsor pilgrimages to Africa as a part of the ritual.

Upon studying the various ceremonies of the Ashanti and Krobo people, I am comforted in knowing that the ceremonial prescription that I was given *spiritually* contains aspects greatly related to the rituals performed by my elder and sister medicine women across the waters and for so many years long before my even giving it a thought. To me, this is a reflection of the continuity of spiritual bonds which know no boundaries.

The Krobo are the most numerous of the Adayme speaking tribes of south-eastern Ghana. They came to Krobo Mountain with their elders and religious leaders and later, due to advancing slave raids and tribal wars, chieftaincies and military war stools were introduced. The Krobo brought with them traditions which include rites of passage ceremonies, or the inclination to create such customs.

While among descendants of Europeans patriarchy is largely rooted in the Christian church, and for middle-easterners Islam may be a common conduit for patriarchal socialization, African Americans who have a strong sense of "the man as head" may have some ancestral connections to African fore-parents who practiced similar customs as the Krobo. In fact, in African American communities, it is fairly obvious when families exhibit behavioral traits that one could say are Krobo-esque and/or Ashanti-like.

In contrast to the neighboring Akan (Ashanti) who are matrilineal, the Krobo are patrilineal, i.e., a child belongs to their *father's house*. Yet, the initiation to womanhood stands out as a most important rite of passage for the Krobo concerning the "life cycle of the individual and which affect a major change of social status." Other ceremonies of the Krobo which highlight the importance of ritual to their society are: (1) the Birth Separation Ritual (the introduction of an infant to this world and its social environs, thus effectively separating the baby from the place from whence it came -- from God); (2) the Taking the Child Outdoors Ceremony (performed eight days after birth, it brings the child in contact with water and the importance of this element to life is imparted to the child through special blessings; (3) the Naming the Child Ceremony (performed by the head male of the house who pours libation and calls on an ancestor to bless the child. He then pours a second libation, invoking God and announcing the name as he receives it; (4) the Thanksgiving After Birth Ceremony (performed several weeks after the birth, this ceremony invites the community to the home compound of the father. The village head/chief pours libation and announces the purpose of the celebration while giving thanks to God. The guests share in drinks, present gifts for the child and mother, and give their blessings, not only for the child but for the village as a whole. The person who cuts the umbilical cord is then rewarded and thus ends the ceremony. The child is officially a welcomed member of the community.

Dipo Season

The Dipo Season is a time designated for "grown girls" to be made into Krobo women. Before commencing the ritual, many parents take their daughter candidates to a dipo priest or priestess to receive a blessing for the ritual.

Next, the elder women change the appearance of the girls by dressing them with certain adornments to beautify them. A Roan antelope skin is used in the ceremony and is considered sacred.

The principal elder woman (called *Yomoyo*) says to each girl while she ties raffia around their necks: "*I am performing our traditional ceremony for you, that you may become an adult Krobo-woman.*" The action of her dressing the young woman in finery makes the occasion special in that it reminds the older women of the time they dressed their girls as babies and now they are being presented as women. Their lines continue and thus, the future is promising for their families.

Leading up to the main ceremony, the girls perform various functions -- grinding millet to introduce them to this important occupation of women particular to their village, making beer -- the purpose of grinding the millet, ritual bathing, practicing their dance, etc.

As discussed earlier, some of the rituals practiced in traditional Native American and African cultures may be too intense for the modern American. For instance, during the final ceremony of the Krobo nubility rites a goat is presented for sacrifice and the candidates participate in the sacrifice. The goat's blood is made to flow upon their feet and other body parts. The shedding of the goat blood is believed to wash away anything which could be harmful to the adolescent girl.

In addition, a ritual almost sure to never be performed in the United States is the hanging of goat intestines around the initiates necks. The intestines are emptied and filled with air prior to being used in this fashion. I cannot imagine a young American teen sitting still for that -- neither would I as a facilitator, be one to handle anything that came from the insides of a goat other than its *milk*, which is rather healthy.

The *Sacred-Stone* Ceremony climaxes the whole Krobo ritual. The girls and elder women parade to a sanctuary. Gifts are presented to the priestess who pours libation with the beer, invoking the gods on behalf of the girls. Candidates are then washed with *sacred medicine water.* Thereafter they may be marked with a reddish powder on their forehead, temples, breast, shoulders, arms and legs for protection and so that everyone knows that they are to be dedicated as Krobo-women. Beads are tied around their waists, legs, wrists and necks.

Nubility Rites of the Ashanti Girls

The uniqueness of the female is brought into focus with great clarity among the Akan-speaking people of West Africa known as the *Ashanti*. They are governed by various chieftaincies and queen-mothers, a term which has become more popular in the west due to more information being shared regarding African cultural and governmental systems and emerging African writers. The Ashanti's National Council is headed by a king (Asantehene). All individuals who govern -- kings, chiefs and queen-mothers are selected from the *lineage of mothers* in their areas. Of the three, the queen-mother is highly favored in her role. Traditionally, she is regarded as the mother of a chief but she may very well be his sister. Underscoring her prominence is the fact that she "proposes" a replacement for the chief when the chief's stool becomes vacant. As the "authority on kinship relations in the royal lineage…" and for purposes of nubility rites, the queen-mother examines all girls who are presented to go through the rituals. Her purpose in this instance is to determine whether the girls have engaged in sexual intercourse resulting in pregnancy -- which would bring harsh consequences upon her. Pre-marital pregnancy is extremely taboo to the Ashanti.

The importance of the queen-mother and the matrilineal lineage of the Ashanti is further illustrated by their belief that a human being is formed from the "blood of the mother" and the "spirit of the father." On this belief the social structure is established. Generations are connected through the mothers' bloodlines. Unlike the Krobo where individuals are considered members of their "father's house," the Ashanti are members of their *mothers matrilineage* from which the genealogy is traced for both female and male members.

Ashanti nubility rites are generally performed for girls who have had their first menstruation, anytime between ages 13 and 20. It is believed that the all-important role of "motherhood" cannot be attained successfully without such rites. Why? Because it is the blessings of the ancestors that allow one to be fruitful. This is the paramount reason for the performance of Ashanti nubility rites for girls and further emphasizes the high regard for the female.

The fact that this "blessing... to be fruitful" sentiment is not unique to the Ashanti and is found in many cultures around the globe is also indicative of my belief that most people are more alike than not. We simply use different methods to arrive at the same place.

Though not quite as involved as Krobo rites and nubility rites of other cultural groups throughout the African continent, there are basic similarities with the Ashanti rituals. Some of the preparation activities of the candidates are almost the same, such as the involvement of elder women of the community, the use of sacred animal skin (elephant for the Ashanti), celebratory feasts and dancing, gift-giving, most notably, the *enstoolment* of the initiates, and a ritual bath.

After the bath, a feast is prepared and food is served to the candidate on plates laid before her. An elderly woman then performs an *anoka* (mouth-touching) ritual with palm wine. Her invocation may be one such as this:

O God Kwame,
Earth Yaa,
Sire Kobi and you thousand other gods,
Today is Monday,
And by your grace,
This grandchild of yours has come of age,
And we are now touching her mouth.
Stand well behind her
So that she may get a good man
who has a name, life and prosperity
to come and marry her quickly.
Let her give birth to thirty children,
girls and boys who will lead
good lives and acquire property.
So that when in the future our grandfathers
call us to their sides, we may get people to replace us
In the governance of this land.
Health to all of us who are assembled here.

In both cases, Krobo and Ashanti, it is only women who bear witness to the final and sacred initiation rites of adolescent females.

It is interesting to note that there is no nubility initiation for boys in the Ashanti culture.

AWAKENING

Once one arrives at the point where one is a candidate in a rites of passage process, one may begin to have a spiritual awakening or experience. Even though the day-to-day routines we all have can be distracting, the candidate will start to realize that she is important in her family, in her community, and that something special is taking place.

She should be encouraged to set aside time daily for prayer or meditation during the period leading up to the ceremony. Either early in the morning at sunrise or in the evening before she goes to bed is probably the best times for her to go into the meditative sessions, when the earth is still and the air calm. In the quiet recesses of her mind, she begins to have a little talk with God. We must ensure that an invisible cocoon is constructed around them to allow for that space where they can feel that they are developing character and transforming before their very eyes into beautiful butterflies. At the appointed time they will magically emerge from their silken homes to bless the world with divine beauty.

There is a buzz in the air, lots of activity, things are being done in preparation for the candidate. She feels a *tingling* inside and it's as though all the stars in heaven are twinkling in celebration of one coming into synchronicity with them. She senses her place in the universe and it is a *sacred* place. To be one with God *is* a sacred place. Once the candidate has an understanding of her own spirituality from this time forward, she knows she can reach that sacred place at anytime through prayer and meditation. In an instant she is there.

How Does the Candidate Arrive at the Sacred Place?

Depending on the spiritual practices of the facilitator and the candidate, the spiritual awakening can be brought about through various means. It can also happen prior to the final ceremony, during the ceremony, or after. The candidate may not even begin to fully understand the ritual until long after it has been completed. In any case, it is a culmination of rituals and tasks performed during the process itself that results in the candidate becoming *new* or acutely aware of herself as the rites of passage ceremony comes together. Whatever has been prescribed -- fasting, praying, meditation, all are contributing factors to the *awakening*.

Awakening for the Non-Traditional

The use here of the term *non-traditional* means practitioners of any prominent religion that gained more popularity and acceptance in the post-colonial European expansion to the west and Africa, including but not limited to Christianity.

In the Christian faith, intense singing, praying and praise of God could result in the candidate *catching the spirit*, which would most likely occur during the final ceremony. Likewise, in many African traditions, particularly, the Akan and Yoruba, animal sacrifice, washing of the candidate's limbs in blood, or carving tribal marks into the skin, coupled with spirited singing, praying, dancing and drumming, can render the same result as the Christian experience. Among the Yoruba and Akan, the candidate may deliver a message to the attendees admonishing them for their deeds or misdeeds, or telling them what they may need to do to improve their own spiritual health. The candidate may also praise and honor someone in the audience. This is when the spirit salutes another evolved spirit which is present -- whether the person *housing* the evolved spirit is consciously aware of this or not.

In the Islamic world, this awakening could be instigated by prolonged chanting or reciting verses from the Holy Quran during the period leading up to the ceremony or after. Buddhists regularly perform intense chanting and meditation as well, which brings them to a state of epiphany. The same is true for followers of a teacher from India called *Maharaji*, who addresses legions the world over. Though chanting is not a part of their program, they use a method of meditation for going deep into one's self and reaching a state of "oneness." Once reached, they refer to this state of serene peace as having *knowledge*. Interestingly, the Dagara people refer to initiation as *Baor*, which also means *knowledge*.

Whatever your culture or your religious practice, if you do not personally know of someone who facilitates these kinds of ceremonies, don't worry, just remember *when the student is ready, the teacher will appear*. Likewise, when a child is ready to go through rites of passage, the right person will be revealed to help her through it. If we truly desire it, we simply must pay attention and follow our spirits.

LOGISTICS OF THE RITUAL

Outline of Rites of Passage Ceremony	
I.	Cleansing of Venue
II.	Procession of Participants and Salute to Ancestral Shrine
III.	Welcome
IV.	Prayer and Libation
V.	Dance and/or drum presentation
VI.	Gift presentation
VII.	Charges to the Candidate
VIII.	Blessing Ritual
IX.	Presentation of Honoree
X.	Community Blessing

As you have noticed, on the previous pages, brief descriptions and some history of just a few rites of passage methods have been given. We also talked about the awakening that can occur from participation in a rites of passage ceremony and how this can be brought about through the spiritual practices of people of different cultures and/or faiths.

Upon *receiving* the prescribed specifics for the ritual to be performed, certain basic elements can be put in place:

- Set the date;

- Select the venue, keeping in mind the number of participants and guests;

- Consult with the parents and the candidate(s) to explain what will take place during the ceremony as fully as possible (if not done previously);

- Determine who will act as a coordinator/point person for the day of the ceremony

- Determine who will participate and how many guests will be invited;

- Make a list of items needed, which should be gathered by the parents of the candidate. The items are as follows:

   1. Table or mantel for Ancestral Shrine;

   2. Photos of female elders or family members (grandmothers, aunts, sisters) who are deceased;

   3. 2 White candles[4]; 3 if candidates are Christian[5];

   4. Sage, Sweetgrass, sometimes cedar, tobacco[6], and a lighter/matches, corn pollen, blue corn, or coarsely ground yellow corn meal;

   5. (a) White dress/outfit for the candidate; (b)a red sash, ribbon or flower may be worn as an accent, or red paint on the face; **and** (c) a piece of leather or several strips of leather (preferably tanned deer or elk hide) or a piece of fur large enough to stand on;

   6. Condiments: salt, red pepper, lemon or bitter-root, olive oil or palm oil, honey;

---

[4]   For the Yoruba, 4 white candles are used.

[5]   For Christian candidates, 3 candles would signify the Father, Son and Holy Ghost.

[6]   Tobacco, for Native Americans, signifies an herb of passage or for traveling on a journey. In the past, tobacco was offered as a gift by strangers when they entered villages outside of their own or traveled to foreign lands throughout Turtle Island (present-day United States). The Yoruba use it in cigars or pipes if it was something enjoyed by a deceased family member.

7. Water goblet[7] (crystal, silver, gold, or wooden);

8. Fresh Flowers (to be obtained by the father of the female candidate), either a white bouquet or multi-colored bouquet;

9. Abalone shell or a large white thick sea shell (as large as an adult hand or larger);

10. White table cloth or plain white fabric or lace to cover the table;

11. A gift from the mother to the daughter (a piece of jewelry, a holy book, an article of clothing from a deceased relative, etc. It could be something new but it is preferable that it be something that belongs to the mother which previously belonged to her mother, thus symbolizing the chain that links generations to generations, mothers to daughters, grandmothers to granddaughters);

12. Water to fill the goblet;

13. A bottle of mineral oil or a purification oil, or Florida Water;

14. A wand made of turkey feathers or a hand-made wand made from large long green leaves (the wooden stem part of the branches can be bound by white yarn, ribbon or white fabric);

15. A bowl of water for dipping the wand;

16. Music (preferably live drumming but if not available, recorded music);

17. Dancers (cultural or modern);

---

[7] For the Yoruba, 9 glasses of clear water are used, in addition to some liquor, wine, coffee or other beverage favored by certain deceased family members.

18. A list of names of family ancestors (recently or longtime deceased family members);

19. A plate of food[8] (from the food brought in for the feast).

- Determine who will prepare the feast to follow the ceremony - friends and family or a caterer (can be very simple or very elaborate)

- Name a set up and a clean-up crew

As a point of clarity, the use of the herbs (Sage, cedar, sweetgrass) and their burning in the abalone shell or white sea shell signifies that like the herbs, we come from the earth but it is not earth alone that sustains us, for the living waters of the earth, indicated by the seashell also give us life. The smoke rising from the burning of the herbs symbolizes the spiritual connection between us and the Great Spirit (God). Glasses of water placed on the ancestral tables serve as conductors to energize the setting. At the end of healing ceremonies, water is given for drinking to seal the healing.

Cleansing

Depending on what directions the prayers have rendered, the facilitator of the rites of passage may give the candidate certain tasks to perform leading up to the ceremony.

In order to prepare oneself for any kind of spiritual work and, in this particular case, the candidate should seek to *cleanse* herself daily in preparation for receiving the blessing that is about to be bestowed upon her.

The mindset the candidate should have regarding cleansing should be that she desires to remove layers of negativity, ignorance, pride, jealousy or any attitude that serves no positive purpose for her.

---

[8]   For the Yoruba, 3 plates of food may be set out, prepared the way the deceased family member would have liked it.

So, from the time she knows this ceremony is going to take place up until the actual time it happens, she should begin the process of cleansing. This is her effort to make herself clean and ready to receive pure divine guidance and blessings. Like painting an old house, old paint should first be stripped, the wood sanded down, smoothing and priming it for a fresh new coat. By the same token, from a spiritual perspective, we wash our physical bodies and clean them inside as well as out while symbolically stripping old feelings of resentment we may have been harboring, and bad habits. We gain a fresh perspective that new life is about to begin again. This is the starting point for the rest of our lives.

Like in a baptism of a young person, she may not understand that this process is a *blessing* but essentially, that is exactly what it is. It is a blessing from her parents, family, friends, ancestors, educators, and The Creator. When anyone puts forth a great deal of effort, giving of herself, her time, her knowledge and her good wishes, specifically in an effort to prepare the candidate for life in the *real world* -- no longer under the safety and protection of her parents, it is truly a blessing and the candidate should be appreciative.

As for internal cleansing, one method is ***fasting and praying***. A certain number of days may be directed leading up to the ceremony. This can help clear one's head and mind about the ceremony. At least five to seven days is an acceptable time period and, the candidate may be directed to do a liquid fast (intake liquids only), a fruit fast (intake fruit only), or a vegetable juice fast (intake vegetable juices or pureed vegetables only). If the candidate has a special medical condition like diabetes or hypoglycemia (low blood sugar), she should consider her condition when engaging in any kind of fast or practice that alters her normal intake of nourishment, and make the necessary adjustments. If under a doctor's care, consult with him/her.

An Every Breath Process

A drawback of living in urban environments and having to go to work and/or to school every day in non-traditional settings is that when it is time for special events, like a rites of passage ceremony, time off either has to be scheduled by the facilitator and the candidate or both have to go about their daily routines.

There is no impromptu ceremony whenever *the spirit says move.* However, it must be understood that *prayer is an every breath process.* This is indicated so the candidate will be in a constant state of prayer, similar to how she would proceed if she were in an isolated place. She is simply doing this *in the privacy of her own heart and mind.* This state of prayer should be sustained up until the time of the ceremony and throughout its duration.

How highly the candidate regards prayer will determine how much she gets out of this exercise.

Ritual Bath

On the morning of the actual ceremony, it is suggested that the candidate be bathed by her elder female attendees or the female medicine person (at least two persons) with fragrant herbs and flowers in a ritual bath of purification. This readies her for the transformation that is about to take place and further elevates her spiritual temperament for this special time. Again, while bathing the candidate, the females doing the bathing should envision that they are removing layers of spiritual uncleanness and negativity in preparation for the candidate receiving her blessing.

If available, fresh gardenia or magnolia are most aromatic flowers for the bath, as well as jasmine. A blend of herbs like sage, cedar, sweet grass, eucalyptus and juniper may be utilized with the flowers, but all of these are not necessary; a blend of 2 or 3 herbs can be used.

The bath can be done at home in a bath tub, a pool, Jacuzzi, or at a lake or a river. At the side of a pool, the flowers and herbs can be placed right in the water and removed afterwards. It is not necessary that the candidate get into the pool, rather they can stand at its side. The facilitator or elders should make natural leafy wands out of long thin branches from trees that they pre-select and tie together. At the appointed time, the wands should be dipped into the fragranced water and the wet leaves gently run down the sides, front and back of the candidate, and also sprinkled across the top of her head.

The same can be done in a bath tub indoors with the candidate standing in the tub rather than sitting. If done outdoors at a lake or river, water should be prepared as indicated above in a couple of buckets and transported to the site where the ritual can be performed as stated above, but with the candidate standing in the natural body of water. After the facilitators or elders have done their washing with the branches, the remaining water in the buckets can be poured directly onto the candidate to finish it.

In the case of performing the ritual bath in the open air, care must be taken to ensure privacy. Often times community laws of decency differ from that of traditional lifestyle.

Whereas the site of a young women's naked body during a ceremonial ritual is not unusual in traditional cultural settings, to the general American public it could be viewed as obscene and offensive, unless those who are offended were schooled about the process. And even then, they may still be offended.

To avoid any unpleasant altercations, it is best to select a place that has some means of enclosure of the relatively small area needed to complete the actual bath, which can be concluded in less than ten minutes. The bath may even be performed with a human wall of women shielding the actual bather by joining hands in a circle or standing shoulder to shoulder if enough women are available. Songs may be sung to add to the occasion. There are African and Native American songs that are relevant for such an occasion. However, if none of them are known by anyone present, in the case of Christians, *Take Me To The Water, Wade In the Water,* and *Take Me To The River* are old spirituals that come to mind.

The facilitator and attendees should remember to have enough white towels on hand for everyone who will be participating in the bath.

The color white is widely accepted for use in ritual because of its symbolic connection to purity and cleanliness. Therefore, white towels and white clothing is recommended for rituals.

Generally, if you are where the ritual bath is taking place -- you will end up getting wet. And, while the bath is being performed, it is possible that other attendees will have their own *experience* at the water. Accordingly, while it can be done in less than 10 minutes, the attendees could become enlivened with the spirit and singing, and before you know it the ritual could end up going on longer than planned. You must not lose sight, however, that everyone has to get back to attend to the rest of the ceremonial duties.

THE CEREMONY

Because there may be so much activity on the day of the ceremony, it may be difficult to remain focused on the sanctity of the ceremony itself. However, for the candidate and the facilitator, it is important to try and keep things in perspective. This is why a logistical *Coordinator* has to be appointed from the outset to coordinate the day of the ceremony. This should be a very organized person.

Logistical questions and issues will arise and will have to be addressed. For instance, the caterers will have to be directed to kitchen/food preparation areas, decorators will need to know what time they can access the facility, and in all probability, neither the candidate nor her mother will be in a position to address those issues. For that reason, among many others, the coordinator will have to be in on consultations with the facilitator so that they have a perfect understanding of what is expected of them and a good indication of the activities that will be taking place.

Once all the logistics have been worked out and all the players are in place, it is time for the ceremony to begin.

Reverence to Spirit

It is important to show reverence to spirit and to the medicine persons performing the ceremony when spiritual work is being done. Pulling together a rites of passage ceremony is no easy feat. Facilitators must have good organizational skills, people skills, and that does not necessarily go hand-in-hand with being well-grounded in her spiritual connection. They serves as a sort of mechanism by which a processing machine works. The action of processing a vast amount of information, sensitivities and energies wears heavily on a person. And, while facilitators may appear to have themselves as well as everything else under control, they put themselves in a most vulnerable state when they open up to receive direction from spirit. Their spiritual protection has to be very strong to guard them.

Jack and Donna Kassewitz of Global Heart in Miami, Florida put together an outline they call *Ceremonial Etiquette*, which is an excellent guide for examining one's outlook on sacred ceremonies, such as rites of passage. While their practice is geared toward the Native American tradition, for the most part, and some aspects would not necessarily apply to Yoruba, Akan or other African or shamanistic ceremonies, the tenets of their etiquette guide could be utilized in most spiritual ceremonies.

Ceremonial Etiquette
by Jack and Donna Kassewitz

Remember, ceremony is a sanctuary where Spirit grows -- it grows through us!

1. It begins the moment you arrive. It is appropriate to bring personal offerings for the ceremony. Tobacco, preferably organic, is the most common and most traditional offering for the land, the medicine person(s) and the host. Flowers, feathers and crystals are acceptable substitutes.

2. Make sure you have been smudged before you engage in ceremony. If you are helping with preparations for ceremony, it is required that you are smudged first. Have all spiritual objects (drums, plants, oils, feathers, crystals, etc.) smudged or blessed by the medicine person before bringing these objects into the ceremony.

3. Speak softly in all that you do there. Remember that even though you may be outdoors, the ceremonial site is still a sacred place of worship.

4. Be careful not to step or walk where it is forbidden. When in doubt, ask.

---

5. Nudity is normally not permissible and you should not wear overly revealing clothes.

6. Think first -- be aware of how your words and actions may affect those around you.

7. Leave your egos outside of any sacred site. Your opinions are important at the appropriate time, which is usually not in the middle of a ceremony.

8. The people conducting a ceremony are specially chosen to do their work. Treat them with respect.

9. There are appropriate ways to approach the medicine women and men around you when you have a private request. First, offer tobacco or a substitute to the person you are making the request from. Next, do not expect an immediate answer, they may want to pray about your question. And finally, speak humbly about yourself and the person you are requesting help from.

10. Profanity of any sort is not allowed.

11. The use of drugs should be discussed immediately with the medicine person(s) in charge.

12. If you are feeling particularly stressed, depressed or out of control at anytime, please tell the medicine person. They can help you address these feelings before they begin to overpower other people's space and time at the ceremony.

13. When it is your turn to speak, keep it short and to the point. Try to go straight to the heart of your intent and state it simply. Do not monopolize ceremonial time with details of your problems; this shows disrespect for others and the ceremony. This becomes increasingly important as the number of participants in the ceremony grows.

14. When bringing children into ceremony, explain the ceremonial etiquette ahead of time. They will appreciate it and so will everyone else.

15. Photography is generally not allowed during ceremony, ask first.

16. When in doubt about anything... it is prudent to ask.

17. This is sacred time... take each step as if in prayer.

The Ancestral Table

If access to the facility on the morning of the ceremony is possible, the ancestral table should be set up well in advance, even before the ritual bath. The facilitator and the mother(s) of the candidate(s) should set up the ancestral table together, just in case something is forgotten. The facilitator will point out what is still needed or she will improvise.

First, the entire place should be *smudged* for cleansing purposes. A mixture of sage and cedar, or sage alone should be used for this. The facilitator must walk through the facility or room being utilized for the ceremony, with the smudge stick or smudge pot containing the burned herbs.

Sage and cedar smolders after it has been ignited and the fire put out. It is the smoke rising from the herbs that provides the cleansing and healing action. Unlike wood or synthetic materials when they burn, the smoke from sage does not set off smoke detectors, and thus allows for peace and serenity during the ritual.

Smudge sticks can be purchased or you can make your own by tying the herbs together (with their stems intact) in a bundle. The tie should be cotton thread, *not* nylon -- only natural fibers. If you prefer a *smudge pot*, abalone shell or a plain white sea shell will serve the purpose, as will a clay or tin pot with a heat resistant handle. The smudge pot should be one specifically used for ceremony. The thickness of the sea shell will let you gauge the heat so it can be held comfortably in the hand while smudging. A thick white cotton cloth may be utilized to hold the shell if it gets too hot, or even a new potholder. If the herbs stop smoldering before the facilitator has finished she must light more to complete the cleansing of the space.

Next, the room should be situated so that *seating* allows everyone to see the ancestral table (or ancestral *shrine*) and what activities are taking place before it. A semi-circle is good, or two sections of rows can be set up with a center aisle leading to an area large enough to accommodate a dance performance, the ancestral table and the candidate(s) and facilitator.

The *ancestral table* can be a standard rectangular banquet table or a round dinner table, or a *mantle* up against a wall if large enough (and if the room will accommodate the number of guests). It must be covered in white cotton fabric or a white linen tablecloth (natural fibers -- no polyester). If a mantle of stone or wood, its natural finish is okay. The bouquet of fresh cut *flowers* should be placed in the center of the table. Arranged in front of the flowers and to the side should be the framed *photographs* of the deceased female family members who are being honored as those from whose lineage the candidate is directly descended, and from whose memory the candidate draws spiritual strength. These can be pictures of grandmothers (preferably) and aunts (maternal and paternal), particularly, those with whom the candidate had a close relationship or those whom the candidate knows would wish great blessings for her.

In between the photographs is where the white *candles* should be placed (and lit just prior to the ceremony). It can be a single glass encased 7-day candle, or, if the candidate is a Christian, 3 candles can be placed, signifying the Father, Son and Holy Ghost. The 7-day glass candle is preferable for safety reasons. Other more elaborate candles may be utilized but must not be left unattended. The *globlet* (made of crystal, silver, gold or wood) of water should be placed in the center of the table in front of the photographs and candles. Space should be left at the front of the table for the facilitator to place the *smudge stick* or *smudge pot, oils, Florida water, lighter/matches, abalone/sea shell,* and any other accoutrements she has been directed to use. The *gift* from the mother may be placed to the rear of the table behind the flowers and pictures, if it is not too large. If it is a large item, it can be placed on the floor next to the table but not in front. A chair for the candidate should be placed in front of the table facing the audience.

The Ceremony Begins

When the time comes for the ceremony to commence, an official opening may begin with music playing (live drumming or an appropriate recording), and the facilitator should lead a line-up of family members in a procession of the participants. Opening and closing a ceremony is very important, as closure must be brought at the ceremony's completion. At the commencement however, the order should be as follows:

- Facilitator

- Most elderly of family females (grandmothers, godmothers, aunts)

- Mother

- Father

- Candidate

The family members should then take their place in front seats reserved for them and the candidate should take her seat at the ancestral table[9].

---

9   It is recommended that the setting be with rows of chairs or a row of semi-circled chairs rather than dinner tables. In this regard the audience will be better able to observe the ceremony and after it has concluded, the audience and participants should then retire to feast in an area that has been set up especially for that purpose. However, the ceremony can be done in a banquet-like setting with tables as well.

The facilitator should take a smudge pot or stick and walk through the audience and around the entire room, smudging everyone in attendance to cleanse them and to set the vibration for the ceremony. The audience may also be invited up to get smudged rather than the facilitator walking around the entire room. If it is a large audience, it may take too long for everyone to come up and be smudged so, in the interest of time, the facilitator could accomplish the same end if she walked the room. For a small gathering it would be good of the audience members to come to the facilitator. It also makes them feel more involved in the process.

Sage

Enough cannot be said about the many uses of *Sage*, an herb which grows abundantly in western North America (New Mexico, Wyoming, Colorado, northern Arizona, Utah, Washington state, up into Alberta, Canada and British Columbia) and in the Russian steppes. I have even found it in southern New Jersey and I'm sure it flourishes in other places as well. It is *sacred* to Native Americans and once you are first engaged by its healing properties you'll understand why and will want to continue to utilize it for cleansing purposes.

There are nine sagebrush species and eighteen subspecies in North America, excluding the seasoning herb, which is a member of the mint family. The most abundant shrub and the one used more for ceremony and medicinally among Native Americans of the southwest is *artemesia tridentate* (art-em-miz-ee-uh try-den-tay-ta), which we call silver sage. It can grow as large as 15 feet tall and can live as long as 100 years. Sage is so pure and clean that it is believed to remove all negativity and filth from people when they are smudged with its smoke. Traditionally, we use silver sage or white sage (from California) in ceremony. Its pungent aroma immediately captures one's senses and one feels the spirit of the plant. It is not an intoxicating nor narcotic feeling. There is nothing illegal about harvesting and utilizing sage as it is a natural herb, totally non-narcotic. However, its healing powers have been known for ages and sage has been chewed to relieve indigestion or used as a natural breath freshener, held against the gums to relieve toothaches, cooked and drank as a tea for colds, flu, fevers and congestion (as it can decrease secretions to the lungs, sinuses, throat and mucous membranes), and even before childbirth. Steamed sage can be applied to body limbs to relieve symptoms of rheumatoid arthritis.

The *Diné* (Navajo) have used *Ts'ah* (sage) as a life medicine used in many of their ceremonies. The Navaho have made lotions from the leaves and used it for cuts on their sheep. The *Paiutes* have created a decoction from sage leaves for malarial fever, and the *Shoshone* apply hot poultices of big sage leaves to the forehead for migraine headaches. The *Lakota* people use sages that grow in the Dakotas which they refer to as *Woman's* Sage or *Man's* Sage.

Garden sage (*salvia officinalis*) can be used as a tea when one suffers from excessive night sweats, and to dry up the flow of breast milk when weaning a child from breast feeding.

Bundles of sage can be strung together and hung from beams in one's home to bless the home and to give it a touch of love from the Earth Mother.

Libation / Prayer

Next, the facilitator will welcome the guests and give an introduction to the ceremony, explaining the different facets that have gone on prior to the day and what is now taking place. This is an educational process so, the facilitator should not feel that she should rush through her explanations. She should take her time and be as clear as possible. Her words may help someone in attendance reach a decision as to whether she too will have or sponsor a rites of passage ceremony for someone.

Next, the facilitator should ask the female elders to come and lay hands on the candidate while she *pours libation* (with water or clear spirits --gin or white rum). To pour libation is to pray while making an offering with a liquid substance that acts as an activator or conductor of the prayer. It is customarily done in prayer of remembrance and/or in honor of ancestors or someone who is deceased.

Because of the chemical composition of water and/or alcohol (with this custom being a holistic practice), one or the other is commonly used in traditional ceremonies. It is the reaction of the spiritual kinetic energy when joined with the elements that compose water and/or alcohol that creates the means by which prayers are offered, delivered *and* answered. It actually comes down to the *science of prayer*.

While pouring libation, the facilitator may simultaneously take the list of ancestors of the candidate and ask that after each name is spoken, the audience should state "*respect and honor.*" In this regard, the ancestors are elevated and honored, and those gathered ask for their blessings upon the candidate. The facilitator may invite others in the prayer circle to call out names that may not be on the list but who, nevertheless, should be paid homage to and their blessings requested. Remember, this part of the ceremony is conducted with the females of the family laying hands on the candidate and thus, *empowering* her with their energy and invigorating her with the *power of prayer*. While this portion of the ceremony is going on, all of the women who are not actively calling out names should be saying their own special prayer for the candidate silently *or* aloud -- it does not matter. The intensity of the moment should not be lost.

Following the prayer, the facilitator may call for a dance to be performed by designated participants. Whenever transitioning from one segment of the ceremony to another, if live drummers are available, they should be directed to play low, steady rhythms until the facilitator is ready to continue. The same can be done with other musicians.

The Gift

Following the dance, the Mother may be called to give her gift and her charge to her daughter. As stated previously, the gift could be a piece of jewelry, a holy book, an article of clothing from a deceased relative, etc. It could be something new, but it is preferable that it be something that belongs to the mother which previously belonged to *her* mother, thus, symbolizing the chain that links generations to generations, mothers to daughters, grandmothers to granddaughters. The mother should explain its significance to the audience, even if it is a new item. It should be wrapped in red cloth to symbolize the blood all women pass in life in order to bring forth life. The candidate must then place the gift on the alter.

The Charge

Charges should be thoughtfully contemplated before they are given. Public pronouncements as to a service (charge) the candidate is asked to perform and her acquiescence to fulfill the charge is important, as it is given *life* when spoken by the person giving the charge, and the candidate is *empowered* by the charge when she submits to that will. It is believed in Native American culture that the act of speaking a charge or a wish puts it *on the wind* and once something is put on the wind, it is done.

Following the mother's gift presentation, the facilitator may call for female family members to come forward and give their charges. Charges may be prepared in advance and given to the female family members/elders. They may be written on cards or participants may be asked to give their own personal charges. Regardless of how they are prepared, those giving the charges must do so with the idea that once given, it is done. The following are some examples:

- I charge you to be a good daughter to your parents, respecting and honoring them. Will you strive to do this?

- I charge you to keep God first in your life. Will you promise to do this?

- I charge you to regard your woman-ness and your womb as sacred and to care for your body as if it is a holy temple. Will you honor this charge?

- I charge you to always remember that children are a gift from God. If you are blessed to have one or more, I charge you to strive to be the best mother you can be to all of them. Will you honor this charge?

- I charge you to remember that you are a mother to all children, regardless of whether they are your natural children or not, and act accordingly. Will you honor this charge?

- I charge you to be discriminate in choosing a mate and allow God to be your guide. Will you honor this charge?

- I charge you to strive to be a good citizen, never doing to others that which you would not want to be done to you. Will you keep this charge?

- I charge you to, from time to time, give a helping hand to someone in need who is less fortunate than you. Will you promise to do this?

- I charge you to honor the ancestors who came before you and remember them and their sacrifices. Will you keep this charge?

At the conclusion of the charges, if someone has been scheduled to perform a solo, this would be the time for her to come forward.

Blessing Ritual

Now, the blessing ritual begins. The facilitator explains the ancestral table to the audience, even down to the individual items and their significance. The mother of the candidate is asked to come forward to assist the facilitator with the ritual.

The facilitator must then light the herbs for the *candidate's cleansing* (smudging) and blow out the flame, leaving only a good thick smoke. She should then have the mother place the piece of fur or leather that has been provided, on the floor in front of the ancestral table and have the candidate stand on it. With the youth's arms outstretched forming a cross with her body, the facilitator then smudges the candidate, running the smoldering smudge pot or smudge stick over the top of the arm, then underneath that arm, down the right side of the body down to the feet, up the left side of the body, underneath the left arm. Then, the candidate must turn clockwise so the facilitator can repeat the smudging to the back part of the body (or the facilitator may continue smudging as she walks around the candidate in a clockwise fashion). Again, the arms, head, right side, then the candidate must lift her right foot, then her left foot. Each time the smoke is run underneath, and then up the left side and down the center of the back. The candidate must turn and face the facilitator.

While doing the above, the facilitator (audience participants or designated person) may choose to sing or hum a spiritual song that is appropriate for the occasion. One that was given to me is a Menominee song of The Mother, generally sung at a time of new birth.

> "A ye ye wa, ye ye wa
> *A ye ye wa, ye ye wa*
> *Tunkasila chi ye ni yo*
> *A ye ye wa, ye ye wa.*"

> Translation: *"Here comes the sun,*
> *Here comes the sun.*
> *The Great Spirit is riding high.*
> *Here comes the sun."*

The Great Spirit riding high simply implies that with the birthing of a child comes the spirit of God and without that spirit, there is no life, much like the Ghanaian a*dinkra* symbol, which translates into, "*Without God there is nothing.*" Other appropriate songs would be spirited hymns or secular songs dealing with new life, regeneration of spirit, honoring the female, etc. Even a positive "rap" could be appropriate for an adolescent who relates strongly to that particular musical genre.

In this transition ceremony, the understanding must be conveyed to all that without God there is nothing, and we walk our life path with the spirit of God in us.

After smudging the facilitator may take a mineral oil and *anoint* the candidate by touching the oil to the center forehead, the palms of the hands and the tops of both feet. In the tradition of Apache White Painted Woman or the Yoruba Women's Society ceremony, the facilitator may then "paint" the candidate with white *efun* (chalk) or a body paint by coloring her forehead, her cheeks, chin, backs of her hands, and the tops of her feet, further blessing this new beginning and suggesting the feminine power she possesses. The painting may also be done in private prior to the ceremony, following the ritual bath. It is up to the facilitator.

Asking the candidate to sit, the facilitator may then ask the mother to assist in serving the condiments, which have been placed on a plate or small tray. She may serve it with her finger or with a small spoon. Only a dab of each is necessary but it must be enough for the candidate to taste and feel the moderate effects of the condiment. The facilitator should explain each condiment as it is served:

1. Salt - for luck. After serving it to the candidate, take it and throw some at her feet.

2. Pepper - because sometimes things get a little hot in life -- there is friction and heat in relationships, be they familial, professional or friendships, and one has to learn how to control the rise in temperature.

3. Palm Oil or olive oil - to smooth out the rough spots.

4. Lemon or Bitter Root - Some lessons to be learned are hard to swallow but, like strong medicine, we have to learn to take it.

5. Honey - for the sweetness in life, and wishing that you will walk in beauty all your days.

Finally, the red sash, scarf, ribbon, flower, paint, or whatever red item has been added to the candidate's attire, must be explained.

> "There is a red river from which all life comes and it flows through all our veins. But, a woman sheds this red water every month so that life can be procreated upon the earth. As a woman, the candidate must now revere that sacred responsibility and appreciate the sacred duty given the female by God -- to have, nurture and replenish the earth with human beings. Gods and goddesses (small "g") don't get here unless they come through the female -- their first teacher on the earthly plane."

With that, the facilitator may sprinkle Florida Water upon the candidate. Thereafter, the tip of the feather or leaf wand should be lightly dipped into the bowl of water to wet the leaves or the feathers slightly. Excess water should be shaken off so that the wand is not dripping.

The candidate is then asked to stand with arms at her side while the facilitator then lightly brushes the wand over her head, down the sides of her arms and legs, down the center of the candidate, then down the back. When she turns back to face the facilitator, a *Blessing Way Prayer* should be read as follows, which may then be followed by a Blessing Way song if the facilitator knows one:

House made of dawn,

House made of evening light,

House made of the dark cloud...

Dark cloud is at the house's door,

The trail out of it is dark cloud,

The zigzag lightning stands high upon it...

Happily may I walk.

Happily, with abundant showers, may I walk.

Happily, with abundant plants, may I walk.

Happily, on the trail of [10]pollen, may I walk.

Happily may I walk.

May it be beautiful before me.

May it be beautiful behind me.

May it be beautiful below me.

May it be beautiful above me.

May it be beautiful all around me.

In beauty it is finished.

Presentation of Honoree

At the conclusion of the Beauty Way prayer, the candidate is presented as a sister, friend, cousin, niece to some, a daughter to others, but to all the world,   (her name)   -- is a young woman,

---

[10]   *Pollen* or *corn pollen* is considered sacred by Native Americans because it is a gift from the Corn Mother, and it is from pollen that plants and crops grow, thus food that nourishes the body and beauty that nurtures the soul.

future mother, and all the good things the future has in store for her.

At this time, the candidate may speak and give her own presentation. It can be a simple statement and thank you or a dance, a song, or some representation of her talent.

Community Blessing

At the conclusion of her presentation, the family and audience should then be invited for the Community Blessing.

As Malidoma Somé reminds us, *"A true community does not need a police force... A functioning community does not need to peer at its members to make sure that they comply with the law. A functioning community is one that is its own protection. And one cannot form a community whose goal is to tear the rest of the society apart."* Likewise, the community that blesses the candidate in a rites of passage ceremony creates its own sense of protection around her and around each other. In this regard, they begin to truly function as a communal family and have the good of the greater society at heart.

At this time, the Beauty Way Prayer may be read by the candidate. Afterward the proclamation, "It Is Finished" should then be made to provide *closure* to the ceremony. Guests may be encouraged to give the candidate their Community Blessing, i.e., personal expressions of congratulations and gifts. Thereafter they should be invited to dine/fellowship with the candidate and her family. They should all be reminded that in their gift-giving, in addition to regular gift items, the candidate will also accept cash, checks, certificates of deposit, endowments, trust funds, scholarships, timeshares or other property to ensure the candidate has a bright and comfortable financial future.

FEAST -- DRINK, DANCE AND BE MERRY!

BEAUTY WAY PRAYER

In Beauty, this begins
In Beauty the day arrives
I will protect myself with this corn pollen
I will protect myself with this eagle feather
I will protect myself with my prayers
I will live a beautiful life
May my children be raised in Beauty
May my children be protected in Beauty
May my thoughts be beautiful
May I speak in Beauty
Beauty Before me
Beauty behind me
Beauty above me
Beauty all around me
I am Beauty
I walk in Beauty
It is finished in Beauty
It is finished in Beauty
It is finished in Beauty

CONCLUSION

As stated earlier, this is a manual for use *only as a guide* towards holding rites of passage ceremonies in an effort to give today's youth a firm foundation from which they can spring into life in a meaningful way. If done properly, not only will the candidates receive a rich blessing, a brief education as to their ancestral heritage and customs, and have their curiosity sufficiently peaked that they will engage in more study, but the same will happen for those attending the ceremonies.

If you are reading this with the intention of actually performing such rituals, remember that healings performed for someone are as much for the *healer* as they are for the one being *healed*. So, when you take on the mantle of a healer or a facilitator of rites of passage ceremonies, just get ready for your own awakening.

Be blessed,
May you walk in beauty, and
May you be surrounded by the power of your ancestors and the love of God.
Aho. Mitakuye Oyasin.

Raining Deer

AFTERWORD

Early in 2003, during the completion of this book, I was forced
to endure another rite of passage. It is a rite that millions of
women in America often go through, from the late springtime of
their lives through the winter of their years -- it can come at any
time. Sometimes men, although to a lesser extent, go through the
same rite. One would think that it would be a rite of passage into
middle age. However, because its occurrence cannot be limited
to any particular age group, we can only say it is a test that truly
challenges our strength and compels us to find the power of God
-- if we did not know where it was -- and implore that all-powerful
force to sustain and keep us. The rite of passage of which I speak is
the occurrence of breast cancer.

Two sisters before me were the only persons in my family whom
I knew had gone through this most unenviable rite of passage. I
later found that an elder cousin, whom I had considered to be
very close to me all my life, had also been visited by this most
unwelcome guest. To my astonishment, it seemed we were not
close enough for this most private of conditions to be divulged
to me. Because it had worked its way into my sisters' lives, I had
always lived under the threat that this cancer might also come my
way. It was of course my hope, like the Hebrews when they knew
the plague was coming to Pharaoh and the people of Egypt, that
a symbolic [invisible] band of blood would have materialized over
my doorway, keeping the plague of breast cancer away from me.
NOT!

Armed with the knowledge of my sisters' experience, however,
and having a medical background, I had the forethought to be
vigilant. Therefore, when I discovered slight changes in my
breasts when I performed my monthly examination, I promptly
went to my gynecologist's office where my nurse practitioner
ordered the requisite mammogram and ultra-sound. Although
the mammogram showed nothing, the ultrasound revealed the
tumor, which was detected in an early phase. A biopsy proved its
malignancy and a standard medical course of action was instituted.

A call for prayer went out to the four directions and weekly gatherings were held in Miami where I was added to the prayer list. Relatives, friends and loved ones all over the country were doing their part -- where they were -- to ensure my healing. Having their support, feeling spiritually *in tune,* and knowing that my life lay within the hands of The Great Spirit, I still suffered continuous pain worse than child birth, more debilitating, psychologically devastating, and which would have greatly weakened my spirit -- had I not held on to the message that came to me in prayer: *This is a challenge you must experience in order to share this rite of passage with others.*

I am thankful for the ceremony of life that my family and friends engaged in on my behalf -- whether they were aware they were participants or not. It does not matter. When we are guided in prayer by the hand of The Great Spirit, the end result will be what is best. And I am eternally grateful to Tunkasila that my best was fixed in the hearts of so many.

As for those who read this book, please take care of yourselves, check yourselves, share your health issues so that others in your circle can learn from them -- don't hide your illness. Let the people who love and care about you show you how much. Lastly, continue to be vigilant and remain in the *every breath process* of prayer.

In light of this being a rites of passage manual for the adolescent female, I thought it only fitting that I share with the readers a poem I wrote that exemplifies some of the rites of passage I have gone through. Hopefully, the women named herein will know how much I have appreciated their love, friendship and sisterhood.

Raining Deer

HOW GOOD IT IS TO BE JOINED WITH SPIRIT IN THE WOMB OF FRIENDS

A Tribute to My Friends Who Are Women

by
Raining Deer

In ceremony I find myself
in a dance called life.
And in the Sacred Circle
I have been joined with spirit
in the womb of friends.

**Retha, Willie Mae, Udee, Annie Mae,
Ola, Cora, Lovie Lee, Christine.**

My First encounter with the Sisterhood
was mostly a blood relation experience.
In this dance they pushed and pulled me out,
held me up to the sun, moon and stars
And said to The Great Spirit
"She is here."

And "She" was stirred,
tossed about, cradled
groomed and stood up
to walk the straight path.

It led to this ceremony in the south.
And, in this dance
I have been joined with spirit
in the womb of friends.

Donzella, Mary, Elvoyd, Jean, Pat.

Theirs were the first hands
that greeted me here, and Gwen Cherry's
voluminous arms wrapped around and pulled me
further into this Sacred Circle.
Gentle pushes and whispering voices
sung melodies without words but
were old hymns to my heart.

The drumming began and
the dance quickened.
Some faces disappeared and
in the whirling about
my partners seemed to change
with each pivot.

Denise, Helen, Talibah.

Theirs was a slow and engaging kind of rumba,
but with each shuffle of the feet
we uncovered layers of history
until the ground was no longer the dust
on which we pranced, but
the Earth Mother who gave us life.
The red clay of Georgia -- called Cherokee Land
was the fullness of her bosom,
from which we gained succulent nourishment.

Wallis, Jeannie, Priscilla.

Yanking and twisting my arm.
Their dance was intense, exciting, beautiful and hard.
"Be my sister, be my sister -- you brat!"
was their song, to which my sweet refrain was
"I Am, **I Am** -- now leave me alone."

They never will.
I always see them, even at a distance dancing
like that Ever-Ready Bunny and
playing that drum…
"Be my sister, be my sister, be my sister."

Iya Sangode, Omi Aladori.

Their hips swayed to a decidedly African beat.
With the smell of incense filtering the air and
the fire of white candles burning,
their dance was of Egun-gun,
to call up the Spirits, to be possessed and
turned, wrenching and contorting
as we sing to the glory of Sango and
praises to Yemoja.

This Sacred Circle is hot and cool,
composed of fire and water.
I revel in the movements that conjure up the spirits of dead
Africans
who are again given life in this
dance of the living.

Aho. Mitakuye Oyasin - *All my relations*
give praise to the Africans who have joined on this land.

Iya Orite, Pat, Jameelah, Naana, Chipo, Janelle.
My sisters, my sisters.

A queen whose white locks crown her head
brought the spirit of Osun to this dance,
as all the women empowering Orishas
surround her.

With shekeres shaking and hands clapping,
the chant: "Egun Arabara, Egun Arabara"
is sung repeatedly and I find myself in the circle of
the wives of the Oba.
It is an honor to be so warmly received and
to know that advancement to that inner chamber
was an open door.

But, the rhythms to which I wiggle
turn me to my sister who jumps with
the vigor of Senegal.
Now, in her creativity, she not only
wears the mask, but she makes them --
only, *she* does not know how well.
There in the beginning and here now
is Pat, ever blossoming into a flower
of eternal blooms of Shani, Kiki and Aquil.

Rabiyah is the child of Jameelah,
my confidant, my sister, my child.
With long limbs like the Zulu,
her dance is wild and fierce, pure and serene.
She gives to me that
which is unconditional
unrelenting and never dying.
The love of the Sisterhood
clothed in strength, adorned with beauty
and armed with fertility.

Naana from Ghana --
a sister-kin who is as close in spirit as my own breath.
You invigorate the earth with your infectious love for life.
Janelle of the written word --
keep on keepin' on dear friend.

Sistah Chipo, mother of Kudzai and Jay. May that spirit of life
that engulfs you rest, rule and abide with you now
and forever more.

Hummingbird the Carib Tribal Queen,
a mother who carries the prayers of the people.

**Willie Mae Bethea Stephens "A.", Pearl Byrd Stephens
and Charlotte McAllister Stephens "A.,"**
I know we really are sisters but tell me again --
how did we get different mothers *and* fathers?
You are the best sister-in-laws anyone could have.

Regina, Nadira, Talibah, Minnie, Dena, Pam -
my girls, my girls. Of course I was too young to have babies so,
your mothers had you so I would have real baby dolls to play with.

Susan and Samantha --
my island girls -- connected from the other world,
spinning magical threads of light.

Lynn Andrews -- *Pulasu.*
you bear witness to the unknown through your testimonial tapestry.
What an angel of inspiration you have been.

Maya Angelou.
You gave me and countless other would-be writers
the breath of life
with your stories - our stories.
To sit in your presence has always been like
going to a revival - smacked in the head
with open palm, blood not knowing
whether to rush to the head or the feet,
but maintaining consciousness in order
to feed from your poetic wellspring.
--Thank you for being

How good it is to be joined with spirit
in the womb of friends.
The mothers -- my mothers
who pushed and pulled me out,
lifted me up, spun and tossed me around.
I shall never be the same, nor will they,
for the waters that whirl around us
are communal and the cup from which we drink
belongs to the family.
How good it is to be joined with Spirit
in this *Sisterhood of Shields*.
We are the Womb of Friends.

BIBLIOGRAPHY

This Bibliography contains quotes and/or titles of books or publications from which specific references have been taken. Page numbers have not been included, mostly due to the author's desire that readers not only go to references noted, but try and take in the entire body of each book referred to which they are led to read. In this regard, not only will readers gain a better understanding of the authors and the magnitude of their work -- be it literary, clinical or spiritual, but they will have in large measure fed their appetites for more knowledge of rites of passage rituals. In other cases, a book may be listed but only one reference or no references were taken from it; however, as in the case with Medicine Woman, the spirit of the book itself and its author greatly encouraged this author to embark on the journey of writing this book.

1. Adefunmi I, HRH Oseijeman; <u>Olorisa</u>; Great Benin Books; Oyotunji African Village, South Carolina 1982

2. Andrews, Lynn; <u>Medicine Woman</u>, Harper, San Francisco 1983

3. Brooks, Phillips; quote from emerson images, Inner Light Gallery, Savannah, Georgia

4. Collier, John and Moskowitz, Ira; <u>The Rites and Ceremonies of the Indians of the Southwest</u>; Barnes and Noble Books, New York 1993

5. Erdoes, Richard and Ortiz, Alfonso; <u>American Indian Myths and Legends</u>; Pantheon Books, New York 1984

6. Huber, Hugo, S.V.D.; <u>The Krobo: Traditional Social and Religious Life of a West African People</u>; Studia Instituti Anthropos Volume 16, University Press Fribourg, Switzerland 1993

7. Josephy, Alvin M. Jr.; <u>Now That The Buffalo's Gone</u>; Alfred A. Knopf 1982

8. Kavasch, E. Barrie and Karen Baar; <u>American Indian Healing Arts: Herbs, Rituals, and Remedies for Every Season of Life</u>; Bantam Books 1999

9. Liptak, Karen; <u>North American Indian Ceremonies</u>; Franklin Watts 1992

10. Pahana and Donna, Council of Light Gathering and Project Peace Pole; <u>You are a Holy Man! You are a Holy Woman! - The Emergence 2000 and Beyond</u>; Miami, Florida 2000

11. Piers Vitebsky, <u>The Shaman - Voyages of the Soul, Trance, Ecstacy and Healing from Siberia to the Amazon</u>; Little Brown and Company; Duncan Baird Publishers 1995

12. Raining Deer; <u>Pulasu - Bearing Witness to the Other World</u>; ©1996; Miami, Florida

13. Reynolds, Jan; <u>Mother and Child - Visions of Parenting from Indigenous Cultures</u>; Inner Traditions International, Rochester, Vermont 1997

14. Sangode, Iya Afin Ayobunmi; <u>Rites of Passage: The Psychology of Female Power</u>; Athelia-Henrietta Press, Brooklyn, New York 1999

15. Sarpong, Peter; <u>Girls' Nubility Rites in Ashanti</u>; Ghana Publishing Corp., ©1977

16. Silver Wolf Walks Alone; <u>Sacred Sage – How It Heals</u>; Wendy Whiteman, Ashland, VA 1992

17. Somé, Malidoma, Patrice; <u>Of water and the spirit</u>; New World Library; San Rafael, CA 1995

18. Somé, Malidoma, Patrice; <u>Ritual: power, healing, and community</u>; Swan/Raven & Co., 1993

19. Storm, Hyemeyohosts; <u>Seven Arrows</u>; Ballantine Books 1972

20. University of Nebraska Press; <u>The Ghost-Dance Religion and the Sioux Outbreak of 1890</u>; 1991

21. <u>Webster's II New College Dictionary</u>; Houghton Mifflin Company , Boston, MA, 1995

SAMPLE PROGRAM FOR RITES OF PASSAGE CEREMONY

Rites of Passage
Ceremony
for

Tamika Jane Doe Smith
Candidate

October 12, 2004
at 4:00 p.m.
Lake Placid Retreat

Raining Deer, Presiding

<u>Family Elders</u>:
Martha Smith Fowler, Mother of the Candidate
Lucinda Ward Smith, Maternal Grandmother of the Candidate
Patience Anderson, Paternal Grandmother of the Candidate
Christine Rodriguez, Maternal Aunt of the Candidate
Elizabeth Thomas, Paternal Aunt of the Candidate
Keliah Bethpage-El, Godmother of the Candidate
Hezekiah Fowler, Father of the Candidate

Attendants: Friends of the Candidate

****

Family Procession and Salute of Ancestral Shrine Prayer and Libation (family females laying hands on candidate) Welcome	Musical Interlude Blessing Ritual (smudging & anointing) Blessing Way Prayer Presentation of Honoree (who may give her own presentation at this time)
Presentation of Mother's Gift Charges	Community Blessing Feast

Celebrate!

For consultations with Raining Deer regarding rites of passage ceremonies, lectures and/or additional information, please send inquiries to:

Raining Deer
P.O. Box 411
Moorestown, NJ 08057
Phone: 856-222-4142
stephensel@verizon.net
Visit www.rainingdeer.com

***

The cover illustration titled "Freedom," depicts a young woman connected to her ancestral roots, the Earth Mother, Father Universe and realms beyond through her extremities. For this author, it signifies how rites of passage rituals can teach a young woman to be firmly grounded within herself but to know that her life aspirations are only limited by the sky. "She" is the *connective thread* that binds the Earth Mother to Father Sky. The uniqueness of woman is magnified in this awesome rendering by Jude "Papaloko" Thegenus.

For inquiries regarding the cover illustration by **Jude "Papaloko" Thegenus,** contact:
Jakmel Art Gallery
2301 Biscayne Blvd.
Miami, Florida 33137
Phone: 305-573-1631
email: jakmelartgallery@hotmail.com

Jack Kassewitz, Pahana studied traditional healing in New Mexico where he was trained by a council of Medicine Elders of the Lakota, Zuni, Hopi, Diné, Yaqui and Apache tribes.
Donna Kessewitz has facilitated spiritual retreats to swim with dolphins and explore ancient Mayan sites in the Yucatan, Mexico. Jack and Donna currently reside in Miami, Florida facilitating sweat lodges, drumming circles, and Peace Pole events through their non-profit organization, Global Heart, Inc. They are actively involved in dolphin communication research.
(visit www.globalheart.org).

ABOUT THE AUTHOR

Photo by Jean Wily Gerdes

Raining Deer Harjo is a free-lance writer and former arts administrator for the *African American Caribbean Cultural Arts Commission* in Miami, Florida. She was the coordinator of the annual *Pan-African Bookfest and Cultural Conference* for many years and co-hosted weekly prayer vigils at the renowned *Miami Circle* with Trinidad & Tobago's Carib Tribal Queen, Catherine Hummingbird Ramirez. Raining Deer served on the Board the *Diaspora Arts Coalition* as well as the *M Ensemble Theater Company* in Miami. Under her American name, she created the format for and served as editor-in-chief of *Southern Dawn Magazine* in the late 1980s. She attended Miami-Dade College where she worked closely with the *Distinguished Visiting Professors Series* and *Phi Theta Kappa Honor Society*. After receiving a *McKnight Scholarship* for academic excellence, she was awarded the *Language Arts Most Outstanding Student Award*. While engaged in metaphysical studies at the University of El-Eastmoor, she co-founded *the Imani Um Nommo Writers Workshop* in 1981. Many of Raining Deer's articles appeared (also under her American name) in prominent South Florida newspapers such as the *Miami Times, Fort Lauderdale's Westside Gazette, The Miami Herald*, and *The Miami Weekly*. A *Leadership Miami* Graduate and nominee for the *Price Waterhouse Up & Comers Award*, Raining Deer served as publicist and public relations specialist to many performing and recording artists, including Philip Michael Thomas (star of NBC's *Miami Vice*), and personalities such as (King) Oba Oseijeman Adefunmi I of *Oyotunji African Village*, and his wife HRG Iya Orite Olasowo. Raining Deer has produced musicals featuring former *Alvin Ailey* dancer Desiree S. Vlad and L. Maurice White. A member of the *Seminole Tribe of Florida, Oglawaha Band* of the Cox-Osceola Seminole Reservation at Orange Springs, Florida, Raining Deer was wed to the tribe's medicine man, Thunder Horse Nokus Harjo (a/k/a Wayne Bowen) in 1990 by the late Chief Little Dove Buford. During their three-year union Raining Deer served as *Iyeska* (spiritual interpreter) for Thunder Horse. A son was born to them, Sage Harjo, and both mother and son currently reside in Moorestown, New Jersey. Raining Deer recently survived a challenge with breast cancer and chronicles that experience in her soon-to-be published, *Rites of Passage for Breast Cancer Victors.*

www.ingramcontent.com/pod-product-compliance
Lightning Source LLC
Chambersburg PA
CBHW051438280526
45785CB00003B/1340